101 QUESTIONS
Adventists Ask

B. B. Beach and John Graz

Foreword by Jan Paulsen, president, General Conference

Pacific Press® Publishing Association
Nampa, Idaho
Oshawa, Ontaro, Canada

Edited by Tim Lale
Designed by Tim Larson
Cover photo by Steve McAllister © Image Bank

Copyright © 2000 by
Pacific Press® Publishing Association
Printed in USA

ISBN 0-8163-1790-9

00 01 02 03 04 • 5 4 3 2 1

To Eliane and Medina,
who provide answers to life's questions.

Contents

Acknowledgments

The authors would like to express appreciation to Milind Borge and Marilyn Riley for their excellent help in getting the manuscript ready for the publishing house. We also wish to thank Angel Rodriguez and George Reid for helpful suggestions regarding some of the answers.

Preface

Life is full of questions. While the Christian religion answers many vital questions, it also provides a fruitful soil for inquiry.

Seventh-day Adventists indeed *ask questions*. They are called to be seekers for truth and understanding. By its very nature, Adventism probes, tests, reviews, and explores the vast domains of theological knowledge and practical Christian living, both in society and inside the Church.

At our Church world headquarters we receive many questions. Quite a few come to my office, and, where appropriate, I pass them on to the relevant department for response.

The questions in this book are real ones sent in by church members. However, the answers do not pretend to be official replies. John Graz and Bert Beach make no claims to offer open sesames or the last word. However, writing from a rich background of denominational experience, leadership, and study, they have provided well thought-out and readable answers to many propounded questions and points at issue. Every church library should have a copy of this book for reference and group discussion regarding some of the issues raised. The reader will find both interest in reading the answers and benefit from the many balanced insights provided.

Jan Paulsen

Introduction

Many questions from church members come to the General Conference, most of them intelligent and deserving a thoughtful answer; a few come from cranks and confused individuals. This cannot be avoided in a large church. The Department of Public Affairs and Religious Liberty receives its share, sometimes directly, other times via Presidential or other departments. This book deals with some of the more frequently asked and significant questions.

In answering these questions, the authors are speaking their own minds and from their individual varied experience. They have done this forthrightly and in good faith, not beating around the proverbial "ecclesiastical mulberry bush." Not everyone will agree with all the answers; this is to be expected. Adventists are people with individual minds, and they do not have a "sheep follow the leader" mentality. Nevertheless, the authors believe that their answers do reflect the general thinking of the Church and its leadership.

Each of the authors has answered half the questions, sometimes with personal references. The reader will discover some differences in style. Nevertheless, because of consultation, cross-fertilization and editing, they both stand by the book as a whole, which in this sense is a joint production. While much work has gone into this manuscript, and the authors have always been pressed for time, it has been a pleasure to think and work together as partners in this book project— each considering the other to be the boss!

John Graz, B. B. Beach

Adventists and Their Church

 Is the Seventh-day Adventist Church too "American"?

She certainly is less American, that is, less North American, than she has ever been. When the General Conference was organized in 1863, the Church was 100 percent American. Fortunately, the pioneers quickly abandoned the "shut-door theory" held by some for a short time. For a few years some held the limiting view that the message had been witnessed to the "whole world" by simply preaching to Americans originating from various overseas countries.

I can remember when the General Conference staff was almost exclusively made up of Americans (we mean U.S. citizens) and practically never was anything but English heard or used in the offices at 6840 Eastern Avenue, NW in Washington DC. Today, the picture has dramatically changed. Spanish is heard every day and so are Portuguese and a sprinkling of other languages. In fact, in preparing this book, the authors have talked quite a bit of French!

So, while the staff is now quite multicultural, the majority is still North American. There are several understandable reasons for this:

1. It has always been so (not the best of reasons).
2. The General Conference is located in the U.S., and it is logical to employ support staff locally, especially hourly workers (bringing in secretaries from overseas would be prohibitively expensive).
3. Much of the staff working in the General Conference complex serves the North American Division and specialized agencies such as the insurance service (Risk Management Services) and ADRA.

Don't forget that the U.S. was the cradle of Adventism. Only after half a century of missionary work did the church membership outside the U.S. pass the 50 percent mark. Today, the North American membership represents less than 10 percent of the world membership, and Brazil is the number one country in membership. We can expect two or three other countries in the next few years to pass the U.S. in membership. Several other divisions are now larger in membership than the North American Division.

All this is a healthy development, but let us not overlook what a powerhouse and arsenal of resources the U.S. Church has been and continues to be. Let us not today downplay the role of the U.S. The U.S. Church must be kept strong, lest we kill the goose that lays the golden eggs! In 1998, North America alone provided over half a *billion* dollars in tithe, and about 58 percent of the total world tithe and offerings. I would like to get the best of both worlds: let us not make the General Conference less American, but more non-American!

 Do we still need a General Conference?

Most denominations are national churches. There are few recognized Christian world churches. The most obvious example is the

Roman Catholic Church. On the other hand, the Anglicans, Lutherans, Methodists, and Presbyterians are organized largely along national lines. The Baptists place organizational authority in the local congregation. While there is much to be criticized about Roman Catholic Church governance, one must acknowledge that after more than 1,500 years the system still stands. We must also never forget that the local church is where the evangelistic rubber meets the salvation road.

The Seventh-day Adventist Church is a *world church*. We have about 100 administrative units called unions (either union conferences or union missions). They exercise a great deal of administrative autonomy but belong to the worldwide sisterhood of unions that make up the building blocks of the General Conference (and its division branch offices).

In recent years, a few voices have been heard calling in question the world-church concept, emphasizing the local congregation, and saying the Church is top-heavy and that perhaps we no longer need the General Conference. I would maintain, on the contrary, that if we did not have the General Conference, we would need to invent it, and without delay!

We are not just a local church trying to save souls. All churches throughout history have claimed to do this. Beyond this, we are a movement with a worldwide task to accomplish. We are preparing a people, from all nations and cultures, to meet their soon-coming Lord. Seventh-day Adventists cannot think just in terms of their local town or region. They make up a missionary movement "from everywhere to everywhere." Adventists are constrained by the love of God operating around the globe in time and space.

The General Conference is the main manifestation of this worldwide nature of the Church. Reducing the role of the General Conference reduces the global mission of the Church. This role includes the formulation of teaching consensus, the setting of objectives, the elaboration of programs, and the coordination of efforts and manpower. It stimulates the vital forces of the Church, helps maintain unity, and encourages the parts to share responsibility for support of the whole, including the weaker parts, and finishing the work.

With a strong General Conference, church action will not operate at loose ends. The hopelessness and ineffectiveness of operating at cross-purposes will be forestalled. I believe in the General Conference because I believe in the worldwide mission of the great Advent movement that is hastening to a dramatic and united triumph.

 Are we a "sect" or a "church"?

We are a Christian church like other Christian churches, although not because we arbitrarily decide that this is the case. We have non-Adventist recognition for our Church's Christian status. First, we participate in the Conference of Christian World Communions. This all-Christian "family" recognizes us as a Christian church. One of the authors, Bert B. Beach, has been secretary of this conference for the last 30 years. Secondly, the General Conference is represented in the U.S. Church Leader's Conference, and the Seventh-day Adventist representative has been on the small Steering Committee for several years.

Thirdly, we have dialogues, or conversations, with other churches. The Lutheran World Federation published in 1998 a statement saying that the Seventh-day Adventist Church should not be considered a sect.

We should also add that we are accepted as observers or the equivalent at World Council of Churches meetings and other Christian conferences. We are recognized by the United Nations as a Nongovernmental Organization, Category II, and are members of the Bible Society. We share with other Christian churches certain fundamental doctrines of Christianity. That is enough to say we are a church and not a "sect," as churchmen use the term today.

But being in either a church or a sect does not save individuals.

Jesus was treated as the leader of a small sect and was persecuted. God can speak through people who are seen as belonging to religious bodies listed or categorized as a "sect." The present truth is not imprisoned in ecclesiastic categories.

 Should our national churches be independent churches?

We have already pointed out that most churches are national denominations. Thus you have, for example, the (Lutheran) Church of Norway, the (Anglican) Church of England, the United Church of Canada, the (Orthodox) Church of Greece, and we could go on. In the case of a number of missionary churches, once their church in a foreign country reaches a certain level of organizational stability, they establish this daughter church in the "mission field" as an independent church.

Seventh-day Adventists have not gone down this road. They operate one worldwide church, doctrinally and organizationally. As the young church in a given country grows, matures, and develops, we do not cut her off organizationally and set up a new independent church, but let her take on more self-governing authority, greater financial responsibility and accountability, and increased onus for support of the whole worldwide Church.

In this way, each part of the global body of Christ receives support when it requires it, and provides in return support where the need arises. Indeed, more and more national organizational units of the Church are assuming leadership roles and world responsibility. Increasing numbers of workers are going everywhere from everywhere.

Experience also teaches that the work of God is best fostered regionally by a cosmopolitan working force that counteracts inward-looking insularity. This organizational principle brings into play various gifts and alternate backgrounds that can counterbalance narrow-mindedness and local weaknesses. Such a dynamic global approach provides a constant reminder that this Church is a movement embracing all peoples.

So, to the question of whether national churches should be independent churches, the answer is a resounding No, for this Church must be a universal new humanity. Any denial of *global mission* cuts the heart out of this world movement, and where this vision dims, the Advent people begin to perish.

 Is the Adventist Church a "democratic" church?

The governing body of the Seventh-day Adventist Church was organized in 1863 in the United States, a democratic country. If you compare Adventist church governance with that of other churches that established their governing bodies in a monarchical or imperial context, you will see a big difference. The word *democracy* comes from ancient Greece and means that the people have the freedom to decide on matters of policy. The vote is the best way to apply this principle. Directly or indirectly, leaders are chosen and decisions made by the members. In that sense, we can say that the Church organization is a democratic one. The president and other officers of the Church are elected or reelected every five (in conferences, every three) years. They can be changed in between, for cause, if the Executive Committee, which represents the Church members, decides. Every leader is selected for a definite period of time and is expected to respect the policies. No one is above the *Church Manual,* the *Working Policy* of the Church, or the will of the constituency.

Yet, "democracy" may not be the best word to describe the Church and its governance in both her local and global aspects, because the Lord Jesus Christ is the Supreme Leader. As God, He is above the people. The Church exists to serve Him first. His law is the law of the Church and is above all human law and policies. The Church is the body of Christ. We are a democracy in our way of working, but we are a theocracy in our essence.

 Can the Church be manipulated by outside forces?

Historically, the Christian Church has been exposed to manipulation by outside powers. Some of these forces acted openly and directly, such as the Roman emperors, Byzantine rulers, and medieval kings. More insidious outside influences brought apostasy into the Church, sitting "in the temple of God" (2 Thessalonians 2:3, 4).

In our own times, some governments have tried to use the Church to support their sociopolitical agendas. Mostly these efforts were abortive because the Church leaders resisted such manipulation. In a few isolated cases there appears to have been some compromise and wilting of members or local leaders under considerable pressure, even persecution. While these cases did not involve changing Church doctrine or beliefs, in some cases they did lead to entanglement with government and perhaps a less than "certain sound" in Church witness and proclamation.

One reason Ellen G. White favored decentralized and broad church leadership was precisely to avoid the danger of inside or outside manipulation. The narrower and smaller the leadership, the more exposed it can become to outside influences. Balance of power is not just good in democracy, but in the administration of God's Church. Leadership responsibilities are to be "distributed among a large number" of men and women.

The secret of avoiding outside manipulation is to keep the "channel" always "unobstructed, that the Holy Spirit may have free course" (*Testimonies*, vol. 8, p. 234). We can be of good courage, for the Church will inevitably triumph; it will not go astray. Christ's promise is unambiguous: He will build His Church on the rock of Peter's confession in Christ, "and the gates of hell shall not prevail against it" (Matthew 16:18).

 Is there corruption in the Adventist Church?

To answer this question properly, we must first of all know what "corruption" means. Are we talking about doctrinal corruption? Is it financial corruption? Of course, it can be both! For some people, financial corruption is the capital sin, while for others it is just a mistake, a sign of faulty judgment. Some believe that the only dangerous corruption for the Church is doctrinal corruption. Still others concentrate their attention on moral—usually connoting sexual—corruption.

Since the Church is growing and spreading quickly, our understanding of corruption can be diversely interpreted from culture to culture, from place to place. Here is a dictionary definition of the adjective *corrupt:* "Marked by immorality and perversion; depraved. Marked by venality and dishonesty." Using the money of donors of the Church for personal reasons is corruption. Receiving personal benefit from church business outside of the rules, is corruption too. The Church has a set of rules against corruption, and fortunately the great majority of our workers are honest and abide by these rules. Despite the high level of honesty, we need to be vigilant. All of us must follow the working policies of the Church and consider its business and money as sacred.

On the other hand, the Church should be fair in paying her workers enough and giving them good medical and social benefits. Saving money at the expense of the workers is a very poor and shortsighted strategy. Bad and unfair management may encourage corruption. Corruption within the Church organization should not exist, and if it happens, it should be promptly and decisively dealt with everywhere, every time! God is the God of justice and honesty!

Is the Seventh-day Adventist Church growing too fast?

There is no doubt that in certain countries the Church has been rapidly growing in membership. This is especially true in parts of Africa and Latin America. In some countries, however, there is relatively little growth. This would be the case in Western Europe and some areas of the United States and Australia. In these places no one would suggest the Church is growing too fast.

Vigorous church growth is something we must always wish and pray for. It is a sign of a healthy, dynamic church and provides evidence that the Spirit is at work. This was the case in the apostolic church, when thousands joined in one day. Today we have, on average, about 2,200 baptisms every day. We thank God for this evidence of His worldwide blessing.

Is the Church growing too fast? I don't think so. True, in some places of rapid growth there will be growing pains. That is to be expected. When there is a yearly growth rate in a given area or country of 30 percent, this does stretch the Church's infrastructure to the limit, but so far we have not experienced a breaking point, because with spiritual growth and vitality also come material blessings and structural adjustment. Yes, there may be a temporary lack of worship facilities, a need of more pastors, and a lack of denominational maturity and understanding on the part of the flood of newly baptized members. Experienced members may question how deeply historical Adventism has penetrated into the lives of the new members. There can even develop a tension between the old guard, who were faithful under trying circumstances and even persecution, and the wave of new members that have joined the Church now that the door of religious liberty has been opened in some countries. However, with the passing of time and the concerted efforts of members and leaders, these difficulties

21

fall into place, solutions are found, and the Church marches on, conquering and to conquer. "Lord, give us more growth, and make us equal to the opportunity!"

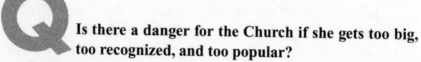

Is there a danger for the Church if she gets too big, too recognized, and too popular?

I suppose theoretically this could happen, and that is the reason God's Church constantly needs revival and reformation. These are the antidotes for the Laodicean and lackadaisical attitude that can develop when one feels "rich and increased with goods, and hav[ing] need of nothing" (Revelation 3:17).

I have sat on numerous church committees during the past half century. I have never noticed that we felt rich and in need of nothing. On the contrary, there was always concern because we were too "poor" and could not meet all our needs and achieve all goals. Again and again legitimate budget requests could only be partially met, and sometimes not at all.

Is the Church too big? Hardly. In most countries we are a small church, and, as far as public authorities and the media are concerned, a rather insignificant one at that. There are countries in Europe (I mention Europe, because outside of the United States, that is where we have had the longest presence) where we have only a few hundred members in populations of many millions. On the other hand, there are countries, fortunately, where our Church is relatively large and growing rapidly. But in these countries, we do not hear voices saying that the Church is too large and it should stop growing! On the contrary, these are areas where the Church is vital and active, not luke-warm. Perhaps some of the recent new members need a little season-ing and growth into the "stature of the fulness of Christ" (Ephesians 4:13), but big-ness is not the problem.

Where is the Seventh-day Adventist Church too recognized and too popular? Perhaps some people may feel that the Church should be persecuted, but nowhere, (and I have visited perhaps 140 countries) is the Church too recognized and too popular. On the contrary, our Church is generally not popular. Usually, she is either ignored or looked upon as rather out of step with the majority of society. It is the majority that is popular.

Should recognition and popularity come, then indeed there could be dangers. After all, popularity and success are hard to bear, individually or organizationally. Pride leads up a slippery slope; the higher you go, the greater the potential downward slide.

So, let us pray for growth, for open doors of acceptance, so we can finish the gospel work, and at the same time may God help us avoid the self-complacency popular adulation can produce.

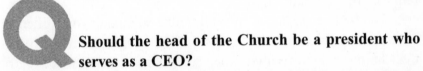 **Should the head of the Church be a president who serves as a CEO?**

First of all, we need to make it unmistakably clear that the head of the Seventh-day Adventist Church is the Lord Jesus Christ. The president is the president *of the General Conference*. Having said this, there is, of course, human leadership on various levels in the Church. There is, however, and must be, a sharing of responsibilities and the need for a multitude of counselors. "Never should the mind of one man or the minds of a few men be regarded as sufficient in wisdom and power to control the work" (*Testimonies,* vol. 9, p. 260).

It is an ever-present temptation for churches to follow secular forms of government. In the U.S., both church members and leaders need, in their thinking, to avoid transferring to the Church the White House presidential system of government. The enticement is always current, and equivalent secular promptings exist in other countries. It has been the age-old temptation to mirror political forms of government. In Old Testament days the chosen people asked to be ruled "like the other people" around them.

When the second century church began gradually to copy the imperial system of Rome, it was only a matter of time before we had monarchical bishops, the papacy, and resulting persecution.

Under the presidential system, the president is the "chief executive officer" (CEO). The constituency elects him and he, in essence, appoints his subordinates. They are there to support him, make him look good (perhaps even largely writing his speeches and articles), but he carries final authority and responsibility. The officers and departmental leaders report and are beholden to him. There are many who like this model. It moves and gets things done. Everyone knows where the buck stops. It closely follows the corporate model, where the chief has almost dictatorial power until the day he resigns or is removed by the board.

The biblical advice is "it shall not be so among you." Ellen G. White repeatedly counseled against letting "kingly power" dominate the Church's administrative structure. What she meant was authoritarian, one-man, or "clique" control taking over.

The Seventh-day Adventist Church operates under the time-honored executive committee system. The same constituency that elects the president also elects the other officers and the departmental directors. They all work under the authority of the Executive Committee, in harmony with established policies and actions. While it is to be expected that the Executive Committee will usually approve recommendations of the president, this will *not* always be the case. Naturally, an effective president will have a high "batting average," and a successful officer and departmental team will hit many "home runs."

Though the president is the first officer and chairman of the Executive Committee, he is not a CEO. He is the respected "first among equals." I have served under many presidents. Most of them have been gifted and dedicated leaders. If there have been some occasional administrative hiccups, it has usually been when the CEO syndrome started manifesting itself.

How should members deal with rumors regarding the Church or affecting the work of the Church?

As everyone knows, or should know, not everything is true that you hear on the telephone, see on television or the Internet, or read in print. What you are told in face-to-face conversations may or may not be true. This applies to both the secular and religious worlds. It is astonishing how many vicious and even nonsensical stories have made and still make the rounds among church people!

The rumor mill grinds away at the lives of public figures, and is at times very active—overactive—in church circles. Some false stories have circulated in the Church over the years. They have been debunked, but unfortunately some are still with us today. Once the rumor has been planted in the rich "believers' soil," it is most difficult to kill. After all, Christians are to be people of trust and faith, not the Church's private eyes!

The first advice to members regarding rumors is to consider the *source*. Does the information come from a credible news source, with a track record of reliability? Does it come from the recognized Adventist media or leadership of the Church? Or does it come from offshoot elements trying, in an underhanded way, to damage the Church? When such individuals disseminate information, and it is true, it is a pure coincidence. If you cannot clearly identify the source, this should raise a flag of caution and diffidence. The "I heard from someone who said that someone told him" rumor has sand as its foundation.

Then consider the *intention*. Is the rumor trying to strengthen faith, does it aim at building confidence, or is it encouraging suspicion and division? Remember that it is the work of Satan to be the "accuser of [the] brethren" (Revelation 12:10).

Does the rumor *make sense*? Some stories are so illogical and farfetched that any reasonable person should question their authenticity. Yes, God works at times in marvelous and mysterious ways His wonders to perform, but not in ridiculous and silly ways.

Finally, always *verify* rumors. The fact that it is printed means really nothing. We live in an age of misinformation. Check with your pastor, check with your conference office, check with the *Adventist Review*, and, if needed, even check with the communication department of higher organizations (such as the division or General Conference).

We are told that we are living in a crooked generation. The divine counsel is not only to be "harmless as doves," but also "*wise* as serpents" (Matthew 10:16).

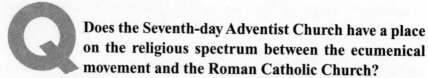 **Does the Seventh-day Adventist Church have a place on the religious spectrum between the ecumenical movement and the Roman Catholic Church?**

It is not always easy to place the position of the SDA Church on the Christian spectrum. She wants to have good relationships with other churches and participates in the meetings of Christian World Communions, but is not part of organized ecumenism. As Seventh-day Adventists, we do not want to be alone, but we cannot share with other brothers and sisters the attractive vision of one united mega-Christian church. Does this position make sense?

We are still a small church in most countries, but we are becoming more and more significant. If our membership keeps increasing without schism or internal divisions, our position will be greatly reinforced over the next several decades, if time lasts, though I hope the Lord will return much sooner. If this is not the case, what will be our role in this new century? Large membership increases are projected. What will be our place between the ecumenical movement and the Catholic Church? Do we have a place?

The Roman Catholic Church will maintain her leadership in Christianity, this seems clear. Will the ecumenical movement be the other pole? Perhaps not! Why? The dream of the ecumenists is not to have two poles, but to have visible Christian unity, which presupposes one pole. This can take a long time to realize, and multiple forms may develop, but the goal of one unity is the dream! What will be the outcome? Will the Protestants disappear? Will the Catholics become Protestants? This is not the real issue. Unity as the goal is the issue, and it cannot be achieved without transformation. A pro-ecumenical approach would mean that the difference between Catholics and Protestants would not produce visible tension, as is the case today. In maintaining its current position, the SDA Church offers a Christian alternative which requires being totally Christian—that is, a Christ- and Bible-centered church, while keeping her identity, her message, and faithfulness to the eternal gospel. I believe this alternative is possible without being aggressive against other Christian churches. We must learn how to be different and not antagonistic, but loving and respectful of others. Are we not following the same Savior, the same God?

To offer an alternative, Seventh-day Adventists should become the friends of everyone, model Christians full of love, and using courtesy when dealing with people. Let us be a friendly Church to the inhabitants of the globe. Let people freely choose what message they accept, what Christianity they want to live. We should never be those who pressure, oppress, or persecute. We are the people of freedom. Oppression and persecution are the marks of the antichrist.

To summarize, being an alternative Christian church means to be as close as possible to our Lord Jesus Christ, and therefore to our fellow human beings for whom He died. This is an idealistic vision. We are living in a world with a global view, and Christianity is attacked from all sides. Islam has one billion followers and is growing very fast. Hinduism, Buddhism, and the New Age philosophies are becoming more popular in the Western world. Is refusing a project of unity among the Christians the best way to defend the Christian faith? As Seventh-day Adventists, we answer, "Yes!" Another question is "Are we sure we will not change our position?" There is always the danger or temptation to change. A Chinese proverb says, "The one who has fought the dragon for 300 years may become a dragon." As Seventh-day Adventists, we have fought the dragon for over 150 years! We will not become a dragon, but there are other pitfalls. The Seventh-day Adventist Church could become a big organization living for herself, defending herself, promoting herself. The more properties, institutions, and recognition we have, the more we will be tempted to become corporation-centered. This we must avoid at all costs.

May the Lord correct us as often as needed. May we become always more apostolic in order to remain "people of God" and "the last messengers." We must never forget that this Church exists not for herself, but for God and for a special mission.

Q Will we have an organized Seventh-day Adventist Church in China?

It depends what you mean by "organized." In China we already have many organized local congregations, mostly under the umbrella of the Three Self Movement, approved by the Chinese authorities. "Three Self" means self-governing, self-financing, and self-propagating. In many ways, these are time-honored Adventist concepts.

We do have a functioning union office in China, located in Hong Kong, which is now a part of China. This office coordinates radio and other work, as circumstances dictate. Relations with the political authorities are not bad, though it is not easy to be on the same wavelength with those espousing atheistic ideology.

While we are able to have fraternal spiritual contacts from the General Conference with the brothers and sisters in China, the Chinese "Three Self" concept does not permit any form of organized control, coordination, or support from abroad. We pray that before too long, normal, fruitful, organized relations will be able to flourish back and forth between China and the World Church, always respecting the local administrative authority of the Chinese Church, within the worldwide Adventist family. We will all be better for it.

 How can we deal with dissent within the Church?

Of course, we would much rather talk about consensus and agreement. Sometimes we are even tempted to place our heads in the sand concerning disagreement, waiting for the trouble to go away or move on elsewhere. There have always been, and, I presume, will probably always be, dissenters in the Church—for good or evil. They can be a pain in our theological or administrative necks. They press to the limit the freedom of the individual. At times they pound on the interfacing door between individual rights (and freedom of conscience) and church-group rights. What should the Church do?

It is one thing for a person to have a private dissenting view on some point. It is another matter if the individual concerned actively disseminates and pushes his dissenting views and even becomes obsessed with the matter so that it moves to center stage of this person's relationship to the Church. Dissenters may stimulate the Church to study a question—and this can be helpful—but they have no right to decide the question for the Church, as some dissidents are prone to do.

Unity is a vital—even existential—characteristic of the Church. Anyone fomenting disunity is involved in questionable, perhaps destructive, activity. It is the mark of arrogance to assume to be right and everyone else wrong. What a dissenter may think is right, the larger Church community of believers may regard as wrong. Dissenters loyal to the Church will understand that even a genuine new insight may not be acceptable to the corporate body at first exposure. There is the real danger of divisiveness. It is wise to allow such views time to mature and insert themselves into the life of God's Church. In so doing, the proponents of the new position show respect and love for the unity and integrity of the body of Christ.

The Church has established guidelines for examining divergent or dissenting views. This is to be done by competent committees. Either the alternative view will be accepted or it will be found wanting and rejected. A decision may be postponed because more time, information, and study are needed. In any case, the Church will have listened, hopefully with respect and care.

We all have liberties, but we also have responsibilities. Church members, and this is especially true for dissenters, need a spirit of tentative inquiry rather than militant dogmatism. The seeds of disunity and disloyalty scatter widely. Pastors or church officers who are chronic dissenters vis-à-vis the conference are sowing seeds of dissent among the church members. Sooner or later the seeds will sprout dissent toward their own leadership.

 Should Adventists go to court against other Adventists?

This is a pernicious and vexing issue that has arisen in the Christian Church time and time again throughout history. The Christian Church is to be a society within the larger society, made up of those who have been called out of the general community, and accept Jesus Christ as Lord, and fellow church members as brothers and sisters.

The biblical counsel in Matthew 18 and 1 Corinthians 6 is not to go to court to solve problems between members, but rather to use the procedures and authority of the church to reach a settlement. In fact, Paul uses rather strong language to denounce the practice of running to pagan courts to accuse fellow church members. He says, in essence, that it is shameful to settle such grievances before pagan judges outside the church, as if there were not sufficient wisdom and justice available inside the church. Christians should make every effort to safeguard the unity and honor of the Church.

Ellen G. White gives similar advice: "Lawsuits between brethren are a reproach to the cause of truth. Christians who go to law with one another expose the church to the ridicule of her enemies. . . . By ignoring the authority of the church, they show contempt for God, who gave to the church its authority" (*The Acts of the Apostles,* p. 306). But in order for this to work, those involved in disputes must *accept the authority of the Church.*

What happens when a church member does not accept adjudication by the Church? In that case, the biblical ideal does not work. What does the leadership do when its authority and the biblical model are ignored or rejected? The biblical answer is clear:

> "Moreover if thy brother shall trespass against thee,
> go and tell him his fault . . . but if he will not hear thee,
> then take with thee one or two more . . . witnesses. . . . And
> if he shall neglect to hear them, tell it unto the church: but
> if he neglect to hear the church, let him be unto thee as an
> heathen man" (Matthew 18:15-17).

In his first letter to the Corinthians, Paul seems to take it for granted that church members will accept and abide by the authority and decision of the church. Jesus goes one step further and says that if members *reject the authority of the church*, then they are to be considered as pagans, or, as we should express it today, as non-members. In this case the logical option is civil litigation. Having exhausted the biblical procedure, and the decision-making authority of the Church having been rejected, the option is to deal with such individuals as one would with any non-member.

There is another intricate point: in recent decades some civil legal matters have become extremely complex, convoluted, and time consuming. There are increasingly complicated tax, property, insurance, corporation, estate, and trust laws and all kinds of local codes that seem to pop up at unexpected moments. It would seem to me that some of these matters may go well beyond the capacity of normal church authority to deal with. In fact, the Seventh-day Adventist *Church Manual* states that there are "cases that are clearly within the jurisdiction of the civil courts and not within the authority of the church" (p.165, 1995 edition). In such cases, there may be little choice—call it a necessary evil if you wish—but to call upon the expertise of the legal profession to gain an equitable solution, including adjudication before a secular tribunal. Such cases may include, for example, insurance claims, custody for minor children, boundaries and ownership of real property, and product liability. In any case, it is hard to see how in such intricate, often quite impersonal issues the Church could be "exposed to ridicule" by Adventists appearing in court on opposite sides, when their Adventism would in all likelihood not be a public issue at all. In fact, for the Church to get involved with a lack of competence, and no adequate process for just settlement, could risk exposing the Church to "ridicule." Furthermore, some of these legal matters are so drawn-out and at risk for moving to center stage, that the Church must "constantly be on guard against turning from its gospel mission and taking up the duties of a civil magistrate" (*Church Manual*, p.165).

Every Seventh-day Adventist should, as far as within reach, live at peace and good neighborliness with all men, not least brothers and sisters in Christ (see Romans 12:18). Selfishness, the spirit of contention, and adversary proceedings are out of harmony with God's plan and purpose for His Church and children.

 How can the Church deal with "new light"?

Are the beliefs and teachings of the Church set in theological and doctrinal concrete? This is not the case, though sometimes it may appear so. As Christians, we have, under the guidance of the Holy Spirit, an expanding understanding of truth. It is arrogant micro-religion to think one possesses all the truth; only God knows all the truth. Without the concept of a growing and expanding truth (and the universe for that matter), eternity becomes a bore.

As church leaders, we try to promote consensus rather than controversy. However, it is important to remember that reaching out for consensus implies *uninhibited search for truth*. We have this exciting promise: "New light will ever be revealed on the word of God to him who is in living connection with the Son of Righteousness. Let no one come to the conclusion that there is no more truth to be revealed" (*Counsels to Writers and Editors*, p. 35).

We should, however, keep in mind that new truth does not invalidate established truth. What it does is add new dimensions and luster. More often than not, the Church will need to work on the plan of addition or multiplication rather than subtraction.

Ellen G. White made the following ground-breaking statement to the Minneapolis General Conference Session in 1888: "That which God gives His servants to speak today would not perhaps have been present truth twenty years ago." Lest this, however, be interpreted as providing freedom for all kinds of rash, speculative individual doctrinal views, she provides balancing counsel elsewhere: "The only safety for any of us is in receiving no new doctrine, no new interpretation of the Scriptures, without first submitting it to brethren of experience. Lay it before them in a humble, teachable spirit, with earnest prayer; and if they see no light in it, yield to their judgment" (*Testimonies*, vol. 5, p. 293). Those who do not follow this prophetic counsel easily become a plague-spot within the Church.

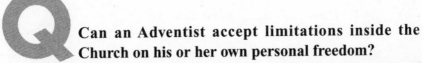

Can an Adventist accept limitations inside the Church on his or her own personal freedom?

The apostle Paul was a great advocate of freedom. He spoke of the "glorious liberty of the children of God" (Romans 8:21). He even wrote the Corinthians that "all things are yours" (1 Corinthians 3:21). That is quite a bit! Misunderstanding Christian liberty, some Corinthians felt that there could be no limitations imposed on their personal free-

dom and that they were "free to do anything" (1 Corinthians 10:23).
Paul explains with great wisdom and delicacy to the Corinthians
that personal freedoms are to be moderated and self-limited by principles affecting what today we might call "the common good." Paul
says to us, in essence, yes, as Seventh-day Adventists you are free,
but remember:

> Not everything is for one's good (see 1 Corinthians
> 6:12, NEB).

> "You do not belong to yourselves."

> "Honour God" (1 Corinthians 6:20, NEB).

> "Try to meet everyone half-way" (1 Corinthians 10:33,
> NEB).

Does your freedom "help the building of the community" and
the interests of others, rather than just promoting your own interests?
(verses 23, 24).

On this basis, looking at the bigger picture, I am happy to accept some limitations on my personal freedom.

Adventists in Evangelism

Why have we as Seventh-day Adventists promoted a "code de bonne conduite" in regard to public evangelism?

"Code de bonne conduite" is a French expression referring not to a legal code of conduct but simply to proper ethical practice in conducting public evangelism. We believe that, in bringing the gospel of salvation to our fellow human beings, we are carrying out a divine mandate, and therefore only the highest ethical standards are acceptable. Anything less destroys the image of a Christ-centered Church and ultimately reflects on the character of the God we claim to represent.

Among the necessary ethical standards are the following:

1. Truthfulness, transparency, and fairness vis-à-vis other religious bodies. When involved in evangelism, no one should knowingly make false statements regarding the teachings and official practices of other churches.

2. When witnessing to our faith we must always remember that

we are at the service of God, rather than of special ecclesiastical interests.

3. When disseminating religious faith and beliefs, the importance of the family needs to be respected, without endeavoring to cause isolation. Adventists need to be seen as pro-family, in a time when anti-family forces are on the ascendancy.

4. Conversion of people and their subsequent joining in the Seventh-day Adventist Church should never be motivated by receiving material inducements or gifts, otherwise conversion becomes a sham.

Our key purpose in evangelizing must always be to draw people to Christ and to a fuller understanding of biblical truth and salvation, not simply to enlarge our church as such. That could be seen as "ecclesiastical imperialism."

 May an evangelist attack other churches?

Perhaps the question would be better worded by asking, *should* an evangelist attack other churches? While he probably has the legal religious liberty right to do so, the question is, should he or she? Is it wise and productive to get involved in scathing wars of words and launching flamboyant cannonades against other denominations? Every militant attack invites a proportionate counterattack. Of course, some people thrive in controversy and spoil for a fight—or at least a debate where they can publicly undress the other side.

Being an evangelist is one of the great calls of God. There is no higher calling. What a privilege to bring the gospel to fellow human beings! The Good News, in its time-of-the-end setting, is so wonderful, convicting, and heartwarming that it does not need a pugnacious presentation that inevitably lessens its spiritual impact. Honey attracts the bees—and the bears for that matter; vinegar is not a pleasant drink. In our outreach, we need to present "the truth . . . as it is in Jesus" (*Counsels to Writers and Editors*, p. 60). Unkind thrusts, invidious comparisons, and negative allusions make evangelism more difficult and close future doors of opportunity.

In the past, some individuals have used a "scorched earth" approach in evangelistic crusades. They get lots of publicity, become the talk of the town, arouse much controversy and conflict, turn people and churches against each other, get some baptisms, and then leave town disliked by most people, never to return. There are better ways.

 In public evangelism, does the truth need to be restricted?

Generally speaking the answer is "no." The truth is the truth, and you don't restrict truth, in the same way that you cannot condense light. However, in presenting truth, we must take into consideration the cultural background, education, and perhaps the prejudices of those we are trying to reach. In dealing with evangelistic food, the writer to the Hebrews uses the expressions "milk" and "strong meat," suggesting that some people, in their capacity to absorb solid doctrine, are more like infants who need liquid nourishment more than solid food (see Hebrews 5:12).

The issue is not whether we should restrict or even hide the truth, but rather how best to fulfill the great evangelistic commission. There is no point in bursting upon the evangelistic scene like the proverbial bull in a china shop. Local people may have been warned and told all kinds of innuendoes or falsehoods about our Church. In such a case, a pedagogically sound approach may be to proceed slowly and in stages, first establishing credibility and sincerity, and revealing honest, caring concern for the welfare and salvation of human beings.

Another problem is the serious lack of religious liberty in some countries. In such places, the public preaching of our message is severely restricted, and at times it is prohibited to preach at all. In other countries, great care and sensitivity, almost needing a sixth sense, must be used. There are countries where talking about false prophets, apostasy, and calling for conversion to authentic Christianity, would immediately result in closing down our work and even perhaps subjecting the preachers of our message and converts to the death penalty, because of what is seen as blasphemy or apostasy or treason.

My father, Walter R. Beach, used to refer to the danger of majoring in minors. Talking about all the individual trees may keep listeners from seeing the whole forest of gospel truth. Once again, Ellen G. White has valuable advice: "It is not the best policy to be so very explicit, and say all upon a point that can be said, when a few arguments will cover the ground. . . . It is a better plan to keep a reserve of arguments than to pour out a depth of knowledge upon a subject" (*Counsels to Writers and Editors*, p. 56).

 Can we approach secular people?

It is of course much easier to approach and talk to people who think as we do. It is easier to evangelize Bible-accepting and Christ-following people (though their "acceptance" and "following" may only be sporadic) than those who have another or no specific ideology. That is why we often tend to orient our evangelistic endeavors toward our Christian "cousins."

There are two major obstacles in the way of preparing a people to meet the soon-coming Lord:

1. Confusion about what the Bible teaches.
2. A secularized mind-set (especially in Europe and the U.S.) that disavows the essence of Christianity and has relegated the churches to the rubbish heap of history.

We have been much less successful in dealing with the second hindrance than with false biblical teaching. We have found it difficult to deal with secularization and win people who ask, in effect, "Why do we need the crutch of religion when we have gained spectacular control of our lives, the environment, and even outer space?"

Acknowledging that this is not a simple problem, how can we, nevertheless, approach secular people? Here are a few simple suggestions (which obviously need greater elaboration into a plan of action):

1. Provide very basic information about Christianity—many people are religiously illiterate.
2. Help people find meaning, and this will give them identity and security. The lives of many people make no sense.
3. Be a communicator and engage people in dialogue. Too many Adventists are great at monologue.
4. Provide opportunities for secular people to meet credible, loving people. This kind of person (not a fanatical, self-opinionated legalist) should make the contact and deliver the impact.
5. Provide opportunities to break out of insulation, overcome isolation, and conquer alienation.
6. Provide opportunities to discover self-worth. An effective convert must discover self-worth before being able to climb out of the secular, swampy lowlands.
7. Finally, provide hope. History and its individual protagonists need not be hopelessly out of control.

We need to scratch where people itch. Secular people "need to be needed." We must do more than repeat what we did 25 or 50 years ago. We need to multiply the services of the Church. It is nice and cozy to be far inside the Church, surrounded by like-minded people, but that is likely to be too far away from secular people. Try standing at the door (and risk a cold draft from time to time!) or outside the door, near enough to God to hear Him, but not so far from secular people that you don't hear and can't answer their disguised cry for help.

 Where do Adventists stand in regard to proselytism?

In answering this question we are faced with the problem of the multiple meanings of proselytism. The time-honored definition has been to convert people from one belief (or lack of belief) to another belief. That is what evangelism is all about. In that sense, *we are not opposed* to proselytism.

Increasingly, often in ecumenical ranks, proselytism has taken on a pejorative connotation. In this context, it refers to corrupt witness, that is, using wrong methods in evangelism, such as offering material inducements (remember the expression "rice Christians"), using cajolery, making false statements, and taking advantage of people. If this is proselytism, then *we are clearly opposed* to it.

However, in certain Orthodox and some ecumenical circles, any effort to convert to your church or belief a person, once baptized into a church, even as a baby, is viewed as proselytism, using "the wrong address." Adventists cannot accept the concept that a person, baptized as an infant, who never goes to church, who has no living connection to Christ, is off-limits to evangelism. We prefer to stand in this matter with a long line of evangelistic witnesses, including the apostle Paul, John Wesley, and Billy Graham. Indeed, "woe is unto me, if I preach not the gospel!" (1 Corinthians 9:16). Witnessing to others about the gospel of salvation in Christ is a Christian mandate from God. While authentic evangelism liberates from intellectual and spiritual drought, false proselytism enslaves and replaces ignorance with subservience to legalism and formalism.

Adventists and Society

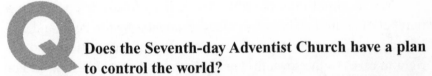**Does the Seventh-day Adventist Church have a plan to control the world?**

Certainly not. We have plans to evangelize the world, but not to control the world. Sometimes voices are heard suggesting that perhaps the Roman Catholic Church or Scientology or Islam or the Mormons or the Unification Church or the New Age Movement or the World Council of Churches or others have plans or desires to control the world. Much of this is simply a guessing game or vivid speculation. There is such a great plurality of religions that it is hard to visualize one religious group controlling the world, though of course some are already very influential and could become even more dominant. The biblical end-time prophetic scenario does envision the world wandering after the beastly apostasy.

Seventh-day Adventists believe in separation of church and state. They recognize that actually Satan is the prince of this world. As Christians, we are not gradually going to establish God's kingdom on earth. Yes, His kingdom is going to come, but this will be by divine fiat and intervention at the Second Coming of Jesus Christ as King of Kings and Lord of Lords.

In the meantime, as Christians we can and must witness in the present about the coming kingdom, not by trying to politically control the world, but by preaching the everlasting gospel in all the world. We will do it by evangelizing everyone and preparing spiritually a people to meet their God, letting God's love take hold of human hearts. In so doing, we will help make a better world, with greater justice and happiness for those who have often been neglected, discriminated against, or persecuted in this life.

 Is it possible to obtain favorable legislation specifically for Adventists?

Yes, it is not only possible, but it has already happened in a number of countries. In Italy, Poland, Hungary, Spain, Peru, and Colombia, the SDA Church has received official recognition, and the right to observe the seventh-day Sabbath is protected by law. In Poland, Italy, and Colombia, the government and parliament voted a law specifically for Adventists. We also have some unprecedented helpful legislation in Brazil, Venezuela, Argentina, and other countries. All of these countries are, by great majority, Roman Catholic. That is an interesting fact! In addition, it must not be overlooked that laws can be passed upholding religious liberty and other rights in general, not specifically dealing with Adventists, but favorable to Adventists because of their general applicability.

Do Adventists need to be more active and proactive?

Yes! In some places, we are following a passive strategy of surviving, like many other minorities. Traditionally, we have not expected to get the support of the "world." We do not like to fight on the front line. The motto of some Adventists could be: "To be happy, live hidden!" With such an approach, we have missed many opportunities to let the public know who we are and to share our values. Of course, we need to follow the Christian method of the golden rule. But we also seem at times intimidated about facing authorities. That someone is an Adventist, even an Adventist leader, does not make him or her necessarily a brave person or courageous leader!

We have to learn how to stand up for our values and rights before the public. We must, at all times, be ready to promote these values and defend those who are victims of intolerance. Proactive, yes, but aggressive, no; accept evil, no, but "overcome evil with good," yes. "As much as lieth in you, live peaceably with all men" (Romans 12:18). Part of having peace is to have your rights respected, as you respect the equal rights of others.

Q **Do Adventists reach for pie in the sky rather than improving the world in which they live?**

Sometimes Seventh-day Adventists are accused by sociopolitical activists of promoting "pie in the sky by and by" and doing nothing to improve the world around them. This is both an untrue and unjust assertion. Adventists do not live in the utopian hereafter; they are not *only* interested in the world to come. In fact, their belief in the coming kingdom of God *requires* them to witness to that coming new world by already preparing a new humanity today.

Faced with the many serious problems of society, Adventists cannot be—and generally are not—indifferent to social conditions and crying human need. Our pioneers opposed slavery and the degrading exploitation of women, as well as the dreadful treatment of many children. Adventists have fought the bane of alcoholism (what has the World Council of Churches done in this area?) and opposed the obscene cigarette industry and its yearly "murder" of hundreds of thousands of people, most of them "hooked" when they were still young and unwary.

Adventists operate the largest worldwide Protestant educational system, with about one million students in six thousand schools. The Adventist health system circles the globe and serves millions of people every year. The Adventist Development and Relief Agency (ADRA) operates projects worth tens of millions of dollars every year in about 120 countries (in 1998 the total aid amounted to more than $136 million). All this is "pie on earth," and in the mouths of many hungry, not nectar or ambrosia in the clouds of heaven!

Seventh-day Adventists believe in distinguishing between the sociopolitical activity of individual Christian citizens, and political involvement on the corporate church level. It is the Church's task to deal with moral principles and to point in a biblical direction, not advocate political directives.

While Adventism will wish to sow seeds that will inevitably produce a social and even political fallout, the Church does not wish to be entangled in political party controversies. Granted, all this will not always be easy to distinguish and the differences at times not apparent; nevertheless, the Church must aim at the ideal and go "about doing good" (Acts 10:38).

 How should we react when our Church is referred to as a "cult" or "sect"?

Our Church can be referred to as a "sect" or a "cult" by ignorance or malice. By ignorance, because people can confuse us with other religious groups, with some extremists, or with incorrect concepts concerning what we believe. A few groups use the name "Seventh-day Adventist" illegally. Through their provocative behavior, they can attract more attention than the Church herself does. They seize our name. A dissident group can publish full pages of irrelevant or distorted material in a national newspaper against the pope, then use the name "Seventh-day Adventist" at the end of the article like a signature. Who notices that it is not our Church? This kind of underhanded activity reinforces prejudices against the Seventh-day Adventist Church. Many readers will remember the name, "Seventh-day Adventist"—that's all. This may be enough to categorize us as a "cult" or a "sect" in the minds of some.

We can be called a "sect" or "cult" by malice or strategy. Our Church is a growing church in many parts of the world. We evangelize and build and operate hospitals, schools, and even universities. We have a well-known agency, ADRA, which helps the poor in developing countries, which can create some jealousy, opposition, or hostility. To list us as a "sect" is a method of marginalizing us. How do we deal with this?

First of all, what is a "sect"? Who has the right definition? Who has the authority to call other churches "sects"? The early Christians were viewed as members of the sect of Christos. The apostle Paul said he was a member of the Pharisees, the "separated ones." Every new group that separates from another group can be sociologically termed a "sect." The early Protestants were a sect from the Catholics, and so on. Most religious organizations are sects from another religion and, in turn, have their own sects. In itself, the word is not negative, but it explains a sociological reality. However, today "sect" is used in a pejorative sense. In Europe, governments have published lists of "potentially dangerous sects." In practice, all sects then run the danger of being condemned as "potentially dangerous." In popular usage, the word "sect" is associated with "isolation, guru, brainwashing, child abuse, suicide, money, crime . . . ."

Secondly, we must avoid *acting like a sect* by exhibiting a sectarian mentality, that is, having an exclusivistic view of ourselves, as better and holier than other groups, separating ourselves from other people, and opting out of society and its problems.

Groups can categorize a church or a group as a "sect," which is the current way, in many countries, to discriminate and to deny the group religious liberty and even its very existence. If sects are potentially dangerous, the country believes it must protect itself against them. Laws have to be voted. Human rights do not apply to these dangerous people. The door is open for persecution.

 Why are there so few Seventh-day Adventist politicians?

A few years ago a similar question was asked: "Why are there so few Adventist lawyers?" The reason was that many Adventists felt that the legal profession somehow had a "shady" side and was not really suitable for Adventists preparing for the soon coming of their Lord. This picture has now changed, and there are many SDA lawyers in the United States and other countries. We have come to realize that law is a worthy and very influential profession. There are perhaps a dozen lawyers working in the General Conference in various capacities. True, there are some lawyers of ill-repute serving questionable interests, but you don't throw out the lovely baby with the dirty bath water.

The same can be said of politicians and government officials. Serving your country and people is a worthy ambition. Adventists have always supported the concept of church-state separation. Some have interpreted this as meaning Church members should "stay out of politics." Actually, Ellen G. White counseled that Adventist ministers and teachers should not be involved in partisan party politics because this could divide the Church.

Today, with the passing of time and the substantial growth of SDA membership in certain countries, increasing numbers of Adventists are serving in parliaments and legislative assemblies, including the United States Congress. When a church represents an insignificant percentage of the population, it is easy to opt out of political responsibility. However, when you are a large segment of the population you cannot ignore your responsibility in political society. If you are not involved, others will fill the vacuum, often with lower or at least very different moral and social standards. In the past, Adventists were told in various places to be ready for persecution from government, and not get involved in the political arena and not defend their rights as well as those of others. The increase in numbers can and has helped to develop an identity and sense of responsibility in a democratic society. Today we have Adventists who have served as governors general, prime ministers, deputy prime ministers, cabinet ministers, members of parliament, ambassadors, and senior civil servants.

We need to point out that political life is a difficult and demanding taskmaster; it was so in the days of Daniel or Nehemiah. If one is not careful, politics can absorb all of one's time. There are many temptations. Furthermore, it is often like walking a tightrope; it is easy to fall. Cooperation and dealing with others is the coin of the political realm. We pay tribute to those who are able to successfully navigate the stormy political waters.

Ellen G. White has left us with an inspiring statement for young people reaching out for heights of attainment in public affairs: "Have you thoughts that you dare not express . . . that you may sit in deliberative and legislative councils, and help to enact laws for the nation? There is nothing wrong in these aspirations. You may every one of you make your mark. . . . Aim high and spare no pains to reach the standard" (*Messages to Young People,* p. 36). As Adventists we are not debarred from engaging in statecraft. But we must always carry our religion with us, not on our sleeves but in our character.

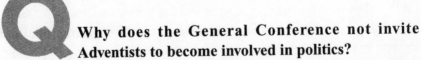 **Why does the General Conference not invite Adventists to become involved in politics?**

It is not really the mission of the General Conference to encourage or discourage church members on becoming involved in politics. This is a decision members need to make individually. Our model and our supreme leader is Jesus. He was not directly involved in politics. The mission of our Church is to preach the Good News and to prepare people to meet God. We do not use political power to do that. We do not want to impose our faith on the world or control governments. For us, "church" and "state" are independent and separate entities. This helps explain why the Church organization is not involved in party politics. Of course, the Church has to take a position on moral issues, for we cannot be blind to injustice, oppression, and persecution. This does not mean that we will favor one party over another.

Having said this, we have to admit that "Christianity is not a religion of isolated individualism or insulated introversion. It is a religion of community." This means that the Christian as an individual may be called by God, or by his own decision, to be involved in politics. We have Adventist parliamentarians, ambassadors, and ministers. Nothing is wrong with that. But we should never forget that the Adventist Christian is a servant, motivated by love, who works first of all for the glory of God, and stands for the separation of "church" and "state."

On the positive side, a Christian can hold a high governmental position, have a good influence on the government, and help to protect the people of God and to promote the climate of religious liberty.

Being involved in politics is a personal decision. Politics can be useful and can be devastating. Playing politics to satisfy ambition of power is certainly not the best way to serve the Lord. There are so many other ways. But God can also work mightily through politicians. Every ministry and profession has both a bright and a dark side.

If we are citizens of heaven, why do we have to defend our rights?

In his letter to the Philippians, Paul wrote, "But our citizenship is heaven. And we eagerly await a Savior from there, the Lord Jesus Christ" (3:20, NIV).

We are citizens of heaven first and foremost. God is our King above all other governments or leaders. The apostle Paul never had a doubt about this. All the apostles who had to choose between God's commandments and human law chose to be faithful to God. John and Peter replied to the Sanhedrin, "Judge for yourselves whether it is right in God's sight to obey you rather than God" (Acts 4:19, NIV).

But being citizens of heaven does not mean we are not citizens on earth. It is just a matter of priority. Paul was a citizen of an earthly empire, and he defended his rights. To stand up for our rights does not contradict our primary citizenship. When you defend your rights, you reinforce and protect the rights of others. Paul was a Roman citizen and had some privileges. A Roman citizen could not be crucified or beaten without a trial. In Philippi, he was arrested, beaten and imprisoned illegally, then released. Paul said to the officers, "They beat us publicly without a trial, even though we are Roman citizens, and threw us into prison. And now do they want to get rid of us quietly? No! Let them come themselves and escort us out" (Acts 16:37).

A good citizen observes the law and values it. When living in countries where human rights are protected by the law, we should be on the front line to defend, protect, and observe the law and support those who have the mission to implement it. The worst tragedy for a nation is to be ruled not by law, but by corrupt power. Nobody should be considered as being above the law! Our rights are protected by law. Thank God! We have to defend them without hatred, in a Christian way, but without weakness or hesitation.

Q Why does the Church not react to human rights violations?

It is not correct to say that the Church does not react. A world church, however, cannot react everywhere as often as a private organization can locally. Every official reaction has to be carefully prepared. I recommend reading the book, *Statements, Guidelines and Other Documents*, published by the Communication Department of the General Conference in 1996. The Church has taken a position on many issues such as the environment, assault weapons, homelessness and poverty, peace, racism, religious freedom, care for the dying, etc.

All these issues deal with human rights. It can happen that our voice is not strong enough to be heard or the context is too complex to react as fast or effectively as we would like. The Church stands for human rights—there is no doubt about that. We commemorated the fiftieth anniversary of the Universal Declaration of Human Rights at the General Conference in late 1998. The president of the General Conference gave a speech, and our guest speakers were well-known human rights advocates. We organized similar commemorations in several parts of the world on all continents. A statement on human rights was issued. We cannot be Christian without respecting and protecting human rights. God gave humankind the great charter of human rights when He promulgated the Ten Commandments. We can affirm that the Seventh-day Adventist Church defends human rights, but we have also to recognize that at times we could have done more as a Church, and as individuals we could have been more pro-active and shown greater courage in a few crucial circumstances.

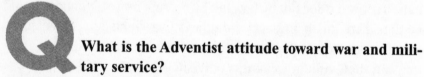

What is the Adventist attitude toward war and military service?

First of all it must be said that the issue of war and peace is a leading—some would say *the leading*—ethical issue in the world today, and a very complicated issue at that, with many ramifications.

Over the centuries, Christians have developed the "just war theory," emphasizing that the cause must be just, the intention must be to establish good or rectify evil, and only proper means are to be used. However, especially since the atomic bomb, a new situation exists, unparalleled in history. As far as being placed in harm's way, the distinction between "military" and "civilian" hardly exists. Modern warfare has become demonically destructive. Total nuclear, chemical, and biological carnage and annihilation is possible. Various populations have already had a foretaste of the far-reaching and disastrous consequences of these weapons of mass destruction.

Seventh-day Adventists promote peace and urge all nations to beat their "swords" into "plowshares" (see Isaiah 2:4). However, Adventists have not adopted toward military service the position of the pacifist churches (Quakers, Mennonites, Brethren). Rather than refusing to serve in the military, the Adventist stand has been to serve in a non-combatant capacity, that is, not to bear arms. The rationale behind this way of thinking is that Adventists, as loyal citizens, wish to serve their country as far as conscience permits, wanting to be involved in saving life and not in taking life.

Some critics have seen the non-combatancy position as "neither fish nor fowl" and opt either for carrying arms or not serving in the military at all. It should be noted that many countries, recognizing conscientious objection, make provision for alternative civilian service in lieu of regular military service. While the SDA non-combatancy position is clear, the Church leaves the decision on this complicated ethical matter to each individual member. She grants historically to each member "absolute liberty to serve his country at all times and in all places, in accordance with the dictates of his personal conscientious convictions" (*Review and Herald*, March 6, 1924).

The case can be made that Adventists should serve in the military only when and if drafted by the government. The Church does not encourage young people to volunteer to serve in peacetime (the religious liberty protection may be less, and one never knows when an unanticipated "war" can happen).

Another issue is having Seventh-day Adventist chaplains in the United States military. Some object to chaplains on the basis of separation of church and state. There was originally some hesitation on the part of the Church, but in 1942 the first SDA army chaplain began to serve. Adventist chaplains have been able to help Adventist military service personnel, and a number have served with distinction, reaching ranks of colonel in the army and rear admiral in the navy. An Adventist rear admiral was in the news (summer 1999) when he functioned as chaplain at the burial service at sea for the ashes of John F. Kennedy Jr., and his wife and sister-in-law. Chaplains in the U.S. military are part of the mandate of the US Constitution guaranteeing all citizens freedom of religion, including those serving in the armed forces.

 Is the Seventh-day Adventist Church opposed to the United States government?

Not at all! The Seventh-day Adventist Church recognizes government as a necessity. Of course, there are good and bad governments. But the Bible supports the principle of government. The apostle Paul is very clear about this in Romans 13. Adventists are good citizens everywhere in the world. But if a government obligates us to choose between the law of God and its law, we have no option but to choose God's law.

There is no reason to be opposed to the United States government, which provides freedom for all. The Seventh-day Adventist Church supports the concept of free exercise of religion found in the United States Constitution and the principle of separation between church and state. Furthermore, the United States promotes religious liberty worldwide. The time may come when the United States will weaken in its support of freedom of religion, and even destroy the two pillars on which this republic rests: civil and religious liberty. However, today these pillars stand firmly, and merit our endorsement and support.

When and if the United States government denies the principles set by its constitution, if it supports one church or one religion above others, if laws are voted which violate religious freedom, Adventists in the United States will oppose such developments. This does not mean that Adventists will become rebels, but the Church would not be able to support values other than those that would support civil and religious freedom. Thank God, the United States government today is one of the best defenders of religious freedom in the world. We should recognize this.

Q **Does the Seventh-day Adventist Church support or work for the United States Central Intelligence Agency (CIA)?**

The Seventh-day Adventist Church has never had any involvement with the U.S. Central Intelligence Agency. Our missionaries do not have covert or secret dealings with the CIA. Even at the height of the Cold War, when Communist authorities were prone to accuse people of spying for the US government, no credible charge was ever made accusing our Church or any of her officials of being involved in covert activities for the CIA or other government security agencies. And yet such rumors have been floated. It would be interesting to know the origin of these rumors. Could the purpose be to discredit the Church organization and leadership? Is the message not often the same: "The Church organization is not credible. Do not send your money to them. Send it to us." There are few innocent rumors.

On occasion, some individuals in Latin American countries—presumably unhappy because of the large growth of Baptist, Pentecostal, Adventist, and other Evangelical churches—have advanced the false and gratuitous suggestion that these Protestant churches are supported materially and ideologically by the U.S. State Department or other government agencies, and represent a U.S. invasion unfriendly to the local "Catholic" culture and history. Except for some Adventist Development and Relief Agency (ADRA) projects, supported by various U.S. and other government-related agencies, and some government funds available to Adventist colleges, there is no U.S. government support for the SDA Church anywhere in the world.

Does the Seventh-day Adventist Church have anything to say about pornography?

It may not be easy to give a precise definition of pornography, because various cultures and legal systems have different approaches to this matter. We remember the statement by one of the great legal minds on the Supreme Court of the United States, that while he might have difficulty in defining pornography, he certainly recognized it when he saw it!

Pornography, originally literature featuring prostitutes, and now simply obscene sexual writing or visual material, is seen by the Seventh-day Adventist Church as both demeaning and destructive. It has become a multibillion-dollar industry. In its worst form of sexual deviance, it involves children. Some claim it is protected by "freedom of speech" and may be an artistic expression.

In our opinion, these claims are largely fabricated to protect those making huge sums from this shameless business.

It is demeaning because women (and men) and even children are viewed as disposable sex objects, not as beings, wonderfully made in the image of God. It is addictive and perverts perception, demanding more and more, by offering less and less, while the morally and sexually desensitized victim looks for greater and greater extremes in titillation, and ends up with nothing.

Pornography corrupts, not so much directly, as by gradually crippling emotions and mental perception, so that the dehumanized individual has little defense against the onslaughts of the drug trade, and eventually risks becoming another statistic contributing to society's falling standards of decency and decorum.

Modern science and psychology have revealed that all our past experiences, all that we see or read, are indelibly recorded in our mind. We may not be able to remember and bring it up at will to the conscious mind, but it is there, and any traumatic experience can unexpectedly bring it to the surface. In this light, how marvelous is the psychological insight—inspiration—of the apostle Paul, who gives this good-as-gold advice: "My friends, all that is true, all that is noble, all that is just and pure, all that is lovable and gracious, whatever is excellent and admirable—fill all your thoughts with these things" (Philippians 4:8, NEB). There will then be no place for what is evil or even questionable, and Adventists will be "faultless children of God in a warped and crooked generation . . . [and] shine like stars in a dark world" (Philippians 2:15, NEB).

 Does the Church accept or condemn homosexuality?

First of all, we need to make clear that there is a difference between "being gay" and "practicing a homosexual lifestyle"; some people refuse to make this difference. There is much argument regarding whether a person is born with homosexual predisposition (the gene theory) or whether this is an acquired tendency (the experience theory). While most experts apparently favor the first opinion, the jury is still out. Perhaps the truth involves a combination of both theories.

It is clear that the Bible (with quite strong language, which today would not be considered politically correct) condemns homosexual practice as "sexual perversity" and "shameful horrors" (Romans 1, Phillips). But Scripture nowhere accuses a gay person of sin simply because that person is gay by inclination, any more than any person is condemned for being tempted to commit sin. The condemnation comes when the inclination to sin is acted upon. There are, of course, gay activists who do not accept this distinction, and claim that gays have "the right" to act out their inclination toward their own sex, and that not acknowledging "this right" is both judgmental and discriminatory.

Homosexuality is one of the many manifestations of the disorder in human inclinations and relations caused by sin. Its proximate cause in a given individual appears to be a combination of various factors, still only partially understood by medical or genetic science. There can be little doubt that voluntary homosexual acts nullify the rich symbolism of complementary and life-giving unity between a man and a woman in marriage.

The Church must open her caring arms to all people, including gays, not in order to affirm an alternate lifestyle, but in order to give pastoral help and understanding to all those who "are heavy laden" (Matthew 11:28). No one needs to feel ostracized from the Church, but at the same time the Church must stand by moral principles as she helps people deal with disordered tendencies. Paul's admonition to the Galatians has a bearing here: "But the harvest of the Spirit is love, joy, peace, patience, kindness, goodness, fidelity, gentleness, and self-control" (5:22, NEB).

Finally, while not accepting homosexual activity, we must defend gays and lesbians against so-called "gay bashing," violence, any form of unjust discrimination, and malicious remarks that call into question the intrinsic dignity of every human being.

 Are any Adventists members of the U.S. Commission on International Religious Freedom?

No. On the U.S. Commission on International Religious Freedom there are nine full members and one Ambassador-at-large, Robert Seiple, who is a member without a vote. Rabbi David Saperstein, director of the Religious Action Center of Reform Judaism, was elected president. Ambassador-at-large Robert Seiple was guest speaker for the fiftieth anniversary of the Universal Declaration of Human Rights organized at the General Conference headquarters. Republicans and Democrats in Congress and President Clinton appointed the Commission's members. What is important to know is that we have access to the office and are invited regularly to attend meetings.

A valid question could be "Why were there no Adventist members on the former twenty-member Advisory Committee on Religious Freedom Abroad?" There were Catholics, Baptists, Mormons, Baha'i, Muslims, Orthodox, Jews, but there were no Adventists. Have we not been defending religious freedom since the beginning of our history? The answer is that we probably do not spend enough time giving information to others about what we do. It seems that Adventists were not rejected but simply overlooked. As soon as we reacted, showing our interest in the principle of religious freedom, we were invited to attend meetings.

This reminded me of the statement of an expert in the area of the sociology of religion. I said to him, "We are not known!" His answer was "Work to be known." We must improve our mission as promoters and defenders of religious freedom for all people everywhere. We should be less "Adventist-centered" and more involved in defending persecuted people and opposing restrictive laws and oppression. We must be seen, not as eccentric inward-looking people outside of the mainstream of life, but as serious defenders and spokespersons for worldwide religious freedom.

 Why do we have increasingly good relations with Cuba?

We want to have good relations with all governments. Our hand is held out to all peoples. Some look the other way, others refuse, and some accept. We have increasingly good relations with many governments, Cuba among them. It is amazing to see how the policy of the Cuban government has evolved in the matter of religious freedom. The Cuban government finally understood, after several years of repression, that the mission of the Christian church was not to fight the government. The Cuban leader, Fidel Castro, recognized that, and invited religious leaders to a historic meeting. During this meeting he mentioned his gratefulness to an Adventist family who helped him when he was in a bad situation. The first time I heard this story, I thought it belonged to mythology! When I visited Cuba in 1997 with a delegation from the General Conference, I heard this story again. It was a Protestant pastor who attended the meeting with Castro, who repeated the account. All this does not mean that Cuba is a paradise for churches, but we have to acknowledge and thank the Lord for the noticeable progress made during the last few years.

Life is not easy in Cuba; the embargo has taken its toll. Nevertheless, we visited churches full of people, and we preached. After the pope visited Cuba, we had a nationwide evangelistic campaign simultaneously in various places, with large baptismal results. Then the Evangelicals had a huge meeting with 100,000 present. I guess the regime wants to encourage a balance among churches and religions. Presumably, it is not interested in having just one strong, dominant church to deal with.

Adventists and Religious Liberty

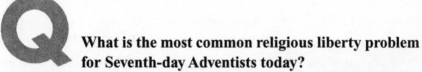 **What is the most common religious liberty problem for Seventh-day Adventists today?**

The World Report on Religious Freedom, put out by the General Conference Department of Public Affairs and Religious Liberty for the first time in 1999, provided a helpful appreciation of the current situation around the world. The biggest issue, which has always been the specific problem of Adventists, is Sabbath observance. In many countries throughout the world, Adventists are still losing their jobs or missing examinations or tests given only on Saturdays. Every year in various places we have dramatic cases. In many instances, the Adventists resign or lose their jobs. Many accept this as a test of their faith or simply the price to pay in order to be faithful to God's will. Sabbath observance can be a crucial problem even in countries where human rights are respected, so you can imagine the situation where human rights are generally not respected.

In the United States of America, the First Amendment, which protects religious freedom, leads to a more active reaction. This is also the case in some other countries. Adventists go to court when their rights are denied. The Church has a special fund and lawyers who are experts in litigating such issues in court. This legal involvement can be good for both members and the Church, but it is also good for human rights. The power of the business or government establishment is challenged on behalf of the core human right of religious freedom.

 Do we have members in jail?

Yes, we have some, although fortunately not many at this time. In July 1999, we had two lay members, one pastor, and one principal in jail. Unfortunately, it took several months to get the information and to have the names and addresses necessary to start working on these cases. We need to improve the communication process. A pastor has been in a Sri Lanka prison since March 1998. He was a successful evangelist and principal of one of our schools. He was arrested on suspicion of terrorism. Being Tamil, active, meeting people, and traveling in a country torn by a civil conflict, he was a target. He was apparently tortured, and he signed a document in a language he could not read. As we write, he is still waiting to appear in court. You can imagine the problems for his family and the challenges for the Church!

In 1998, two members were arrested in the Cape Verde Islands after several Catholic churches were desecrated. They were arrested because they were Adventists. They were beaten and spent one year in prison. Finally, the court clearly held that they were innocent. It would appear the police forced witnesses and tried to create evidence against them. At the beginning of this tragedy, the media accused the SDA Church of encouraging its members to desecrate Catholic churches. You can imagine the reaction of the Catholic population to this information! Fortunately, the Catholic hierarchy and the authorities were very helpful and calmed the people. During the trial, the media were in favor of our brothers, and the court judged them "not guilty."

The fourth case is mysterious. It took one year to get the information. We know that a director of an Adventist school in Ethiopia has been arrested. He has been in prison for one year with no evidence against him. No trial! Silence! We are trying to get more information. It is apparently not a religious freedom issue as such.

 Is religious liberty simply _a_ human right?

There is a tendency today to view religious liberty as one of the human rights. This is the approach of the secular mind but also promoted in ecumenical circles. Secularists and humanists refuse to recognize religious belief as something apart and above other human activities. This is, of course, quite understandable in an ideological framework where God does not exist in reality.

Actually, religious liberty is _the_ fundamental human right that undergirds and lifts up all human rights. It is a unique right. Human rights have a horizontal dimension, in that they deal with person-to-person relations. However, religious liberty, in addition, also has a vertical dimension reaching God-ward. It deals with the ordinary and the extraordinary, the natural and the supernatural.

It is true to say that religious liberty overlaps with other human rights. Take, for example, freedom of speech, freedom of assembly, or freedom of the press. In supporting human rights in general, one helps very often to create a favorable religious liberty climate. However, when religious liberty loses its special and distinctive status, it can easily become neglected or even shut down in a frenzy of contention over other human-rights, nation-building, and national or international controversies.

Why is the Seventh-day Adventist Church defending religious freedom?

As a Church, we can give six reasons for defending religious freedom.

1. Religious freedom is threatened more and more in many countries.
2. Religious freedom is a basic human right, and we strongly support human rights.

We could stop at this point and say that these are enough to justify our commitment. But there are more reasons. As Christians, SDAs defend, protect, and promote religious freedom for four additional reasons:

3. Freedom, and religious freedom in particular, are gifts from God. God created us free to make our own choices. He gave us freedom to say "yes" or "no" because He does not force us to love Him. He wants to have a true relationship of love with us.
4. Religious freedom is a gift from our pioneers. The first gift came from James White in 1851, twelve years before our Church was organized. Then, all our pioneers, including Ellen White, took a strong stand for this principle and urged that we should hold high the banner of religious liberty (see *Testimonies,* vol. 6, p. 402).
5. Religious freedom is linked to the proclamation of the gospel. Without religious freedom, it is difficult to evangelize.
6. There is the prophetic mission of the Church in the last days. Our pioneers were convinced that we, as a Church, have a special role in defending religious freedom. They were also convinced that religious freedom would become a key issue at the end of time. This is still our position today.

Why are Islamic countries against Christianity?

It has always been hard for Islamic nations to treat all religions equally. In the best cases, they have accepted and respected other faiths as the prophet Muhammad recommended. Jews and Christians (as people of the Book) were protected by the Islamic conquerors, but Christians and Jews were considered second-class citizens. After World War II, a non-religious ideology prevailed in several countries where Islam dominated. Christians could be accepted as more or less equal. However, traditional anti-Christianity, which was never eliminated, emerged again during the East/West stand-off. The United States' support of the state of Israel complicated the whole situation. When Islamic extremists took over the government in Iran, Islam became a strong factor of identification for millions of people, especially the poorer masses.

There are also historical roots. Christians and Muslims have a long history of wars. Christianity, with its murderous crusades many centuries ago, is not really seen as a religion of angels on earth. For Muslims, the Christian countries have lost their faith and morality. They have destroyed family life, moral purity, and integrity and have no message to communicate except to "make money"—materialism. The misunderstanding between the two religions is huge. Christians are seen as alcohol drinkers, pork eaters (an abomination for Muslims), and sex-crazed people. Then Christians, especially Evangelicals who are identified with the United States, are perceived as Americans trying to convert Muslims, an aggression of the worst kind. If you are a Muslim, you cannot be converted and you cannot leave Islam, for this is apostasy. In Islamic law apostasy and, therefore, conversion to Christianity is punishable by death.

As Christians, we should not forget that Christendom followed similar principles for centuries. The Christian religion acted even worse in several countries where only Roman Catholics were allowed to live. Luther and the Christians of his time were not really tolerant of Jews and Muslims. In history, Islam was often more tolerant toward Jews and Christians than was Christianity toward Jews and Muslims.

 Do we have Church members in Saudi Arabia?

We have no Adventist church in Saudi Arabia, for the simple reason that all Christian churches are prohibited. Therefore, we have no registered members. However, we probably have members among the large expatriate population working in Saudi Arabia. If you read the *Religious Freedom World Report 1999,* you will see Saudi Arabia is listed in "Category 5." Non-Muslim religions are forbidden in this country. In fact, even some Muslim religious communities are not permitted. Foreign workers and diplomats have no right to pray together, to study the Bible in groups, or to organize a religious service with a minister. It sounds unbelievable, but it is true that during the Gulf War, the American army chaplains stationed with the US troops in Saudi Arabia, in order to protect that country, were not allowed to wear the small regulation Christian cross on their uniforms!

Every year foreigners are expelled or put in prison because they shared their faith. However, do not expect that the Western countries, including the United States of America, will exert serious and firm pressure to eliminate such religious intolerance. Saudi Arabia is, in other ways, a good ally and a strong commercial partner, especially with a vast source of oil. The rich Saudis build mosques everywhere in the world but do not allow even one Christian church to exist "at home." The Italian government allowed them to finance and build a huge mosque for worship in Rome. But the president of the Republic of Italy, as he pointed out, has no right to organize in Saudi Arabia a religious service with a priest.

Is there religious liberty inside the Seventh-day Adventist Church?

From the earliest days of their history, Seventh-day Adventists have been strong proponents of religious liberty, for the simple reason that God asks for and can only accept an homage that is freely given. However, little has been said or written about religious liberty inside the Church.

In the *Church Manual* (which can only be changed by a General Conference Session) and the *General Conference Working Policy*, there is nothing specifically written about freedom of conscience or academic freedom within the Church. But there are a number of statements dealing with the authority and unity of the Church and the related need for harmonized loyalty. Among the eleven grievous sins subject to church discipline, the *Church Manual* lists as number one denial of the cardinal doctrines or teaching contrary to them. Numbers seven and eight are taking part in a divisive or disloyal movement or organization and "persistent refusal" to recognize properly constituted church authority.

It is obvious to me that church leaders are pragmatically more concerned with *unity* than *liberty* within the Church. I'm reminded of a statement made by Winston Churchill: "I was not appointed Her Majesty's first Minister to preside over the dismemberment of the British Empire."

Of course, a church is a different matter than civil society. Since the church is a *voluntary* society, anyone who feels restricted is free to leave, and, it must be pointed out, "without opprobrium" or damnation. The Seventh-day Adventist Church is not one of those authoritarian churches that decides only its members can be saved, but rather leaves this decision to Almighty God.

Freedom of conscience per se is not limited within the Church, but the exteriorization of beliefs (or lack of beliefs) through acts has some limits. The Church and its institutions, thank God, do not have an inquisition office delving into the consciences and private beliefs of pastors, teachers, and members. It is only when a member's actions impinge on the freedom and well-being of the Church that discipline may come into play.

Scripture indicates that deceptive and false teachings can arise within the church. Therefore, it is the duty of church leaders to protect the Church by not receiving false or divisive views or allowing them to be fostered or promoted within the Church. In the case of new interpretations, they are first to be submitted to the judgment of experienced brethren, for "in the multitude of counselors there is safety" (Proverbs 11:14) Is it not intellectually arrogant for a church member to assume to be right and everyone else wrong?

Some views are not crucial for the existence and integrity of the Church. These questions may be of ethical importance, but the Church leaves the matter largely to the individual conscience. Such issues can include most science or technology, party politics, abortion, the bearing of arms, some forms of Sabbath observance, some biblical and prophetic interpretations, church architecture, and some forms of worship. There is considerable internal liberty here.

However, there are beliefs, essentially the 27 Fundamental Beliefs, that cannot be compromised without destroying the gospel as understood by the Seventh-day Adventist Church, and eventually undermining and destroying the Church herself. That is the bottom line with internal religious liberty. The Church has the right and the responsibility to maintain her own nature and very existence. No member has the right, while remaining a member, to teach as truth what is contrary to the fundamental truths that make this Church.

 Why have extremist Hindus attacked Christians?

India is a country of close to one billion inhabitants. It is a great country where the International Religious Liberty Association (IRLA) has organized two international religious liberty conferences. People believe India is one of the most tolerant countries in the world. There are so many religions, tribes, and languages that intolerance could destroy the nation. India has also been the field of bloody religious conflicts, especially between Hindus and Muslims, soon after independence. The dream of Mahatma Gandhi was challenged by a quasi-religious war.

The opposition between Hindus and Christians has not been so pronounced, but since 1998, things have taken a turn for the worse. Christians have been targeted and attacked by some Hindu extremists. In one year, about one hundred attacks against Christians and Christian churches were recorded, which is more than during the previous four decades. On January 23, 1999, the missionary Graham Staines, 58, and his two sons, Philip, 10, and Timothy, 8, were burned alive by Hindu extremists in the village of Manoharpan. What a change! In fairness, it must be said that in his 1997 report to the United Nations Economic and Social Council, Professor Amor, the United Nations Special Rapporteur on Religious Intolerance, wrote about India: "The situation of the Christian community is, in general, satisfactory" (E/CN/1997/Add.1. p. 15).

Hindu extremists, like extremists everywhere, claim to defend their country, their culture, and their religion against Christian proselyting aggression. The Christian community has consistently denied involvement in the conversion of low-caste Hindus and tribal people by force or under pressure. Gandhi wanted to build an India that would not be wholly Hindu, wholly Christian, or wholly Muslim, but "wholly tolerant with its religions working side by side with one another" (quoted by the President of India on January 25, 1999 in his "President's Address to the Nation on the eve of Republic Day"; Embassy of India Press, *Information & Culture*, p. 3).

India is just the most recent example of religious extremists having an influence on politics and creating trouble, discrimination, and persecution for religious minorities. Belligerent extremism and intolerance cannot be accepted, for they poison the atmosphere and bring discomfort and pain to all.

 Why is the International Religious Liberty Associaion (IRLA) non-sectarian?

It was very clear from the beginning of the IRLA that the organization should work with others to defend religious freedom. Leaders of the Seventh-day Adventist Church organized the IRLA in 1893 with a non-sectarian vision. It is both a privilege and encouragement for us to work with non-Adventists on the IRLA Board and on the Board of Experts. This helps give credibility to the organization. As a result, Adventists also serve on boards of other religious liberty organizations.

During the summer of 1998, the IRLA had representatives at the Oslo Conference on Religious Freedom. It was a big event organized with the support of the government of Norway. The president and the co-president of the Conference were associated with the IRLA. One evening, a few participants were invited to a dinner at the residence of the Bishop of Oslo, president of the Conference. When he introduced us, he underlined his membership in the IRLA and added, "It is remarkable to see how a Church, which is not known for its ecumenism, has organized and supported such an open association to defend religious freedom." Religious authorities, well-known scholars, and ministers of government were present.

The IRLA is a non-sectarian association supported by the General Conference. It is a significant contribution—our gift—to the world. The organization has 50 national chapters with a goal to double this figure. We are developing an effective network of correspondents in 200 countries. The IRLA organizes world and regional congresses, conferences, symposiums, and meetings of experts, while national chapters conduct similar activities. The IRLA is recognized at the United Nations in New York, at the OSCE, and at the U.S. Department of State. Governments have asked the IRLA to organize symposiums in their countries and to give advice on specific matters.

The IRLA has a team of experts who are among the best in the world. In an editorial in *The Journal of Church and State* (Spring 1998, volume 40, p. 28), Derek H. Davis mentioned three human-rights associations that monitor abuses around the world: "Human Rights Watch; Christian Solidarity International, and the International Religious Liberty Association." *Christianity Today* published a full page about the IRLA World Congress in Rio de Janeiro in June 1997.

We should also add that when we travel, in many countries we are treated as VIPs because we are IRLA officers. If we could get more interest and support, especially from Adventists in North America, in a few years we could become the recognized number-one religious freedom association in the world. Founded by North American Adventists, supported by our pioneers, the IRLA is increasingly well known and respected in a number of countries. American Adventists need to rediscover this association and strongly support it.

Is the pope the greatest current threat to religious liberty?

If one looks back in history, one has to acknowledge that a number of Catholic pontiffs were hostile to religious liberty and played a persecuting role, often combining political oppression with vigorous efforts to stamp out heresy.

However, today we are faced with the present reality that Pope John Paul II is one of the world's leading and most influential advocates of human rights, the protection of minorities, and a strong spokesperson for religious freedom. He has spoken and written numerous statements supporting religious liberty, in harmony with the

Religious Liberty Declaration of the Second Vatican Council (1965) and the new *Catechism of the Catholic Church* (1994). This document states, "The *right to the exercise of freedom*, especially in moral and religious matters, is an inalienable requirement of the dignity of the human person. This right must be recognized and protected by civil authority within the limits of the common good and public order" (p. 482, par. 1738). Of course, it doesn't seem that the age and precarious health of this pope will allow him to long play a future role. Where will his successor stand?

The greatest current threats to religious liberty come from religious fundamentalism; no acceptance of opposing views; extreme nationalism tied to religion; closed borders to foreign religion; and anti-religious "laicity" (a French term which means allowing for no or little respect for religious conscience out of step with majority practice).

 In 1997, an Adventist couple was pounced upon and killed by a mob in the country of Dagestan. Was this a religious liberty issue?

Yes! But most of the time religious persecution involves other aspects. In this case, we could see the work of Muslim fanatics. What they did in Dagestan, religious fanatics have done in Pakistan, Indonesia, India, and elsewhere. No country can consider itself immune from such tragedies. What happened in Dagestan?

First, In the small republic of Dagestan, Christians tried to share their faith. A few Muslims became Christians. The fanatics reacted with angry propaganda against Christians.

Second, it seems that several children and a young girl disappeared, creating a climate of insecurity and fear. The fanatics used this to focus hatred on the few Christians. (Do you remember how Christians in Europe used to focus on gypsies in similar circumstances?) Someone saw a car near where the young girl had disappeared. We are told the license plate was similar to the one of our brother who was killed. Before becoming a Christian, he had spent some time in prison, though he always affirmed his innocence. He became a Christian and married a Christian Russian woman, and both shared their faith. They were threatened several times and needed to move to another village, but did not stop sharing their new faith. One day a group of people arrested, or rather "kidnapped," the couple, beat, and tortured them. Two days later they brought them to the public square. Were they still alive? Someone poured a can of gasoline on them and set them on fire. About 5,000 people attended and applauded this criminal act. The local TV recorded the event for the news. No evidence! No trial! We reacted, but did this in a way that protected the rest of our people from violence. But one brother and sister have been murdered, and nobody has been arrested. The murderers are free.

A Muslim leader there was very helpful to our Church. He opened the TV station to let our pastor introduce our beliefs to the public. We are told that the Muslim man was killed a few months later.

The people who gathered in the public square did not applaud because a Christian couple was burned. They probably believed they were acting for a just cause and punishing a traitor, thus giving a strong warning to those who might be tempted to become Christians. I hope one day we will be able to know the whole story.

Unfortunately, this tragedy raised many rumors. We received e-mail information that was totally inaccurate, to the effect that general persecution in Russia against the Adventists had just begun and all Adventists in Russia were in extreme danger, as a slaughter was planned against them. Fortunately, some members asked questions at the right time and to the right people. Our team in Russia did a great work. Rumors do not help at all, and people can be manipulated by rumors. If we use rumors as if they were truth, we are discredited and people lose their confidence in us. We must be serious and honest. Some try to use rumors to prove a prophetic interpretation. It is not an effective way to prove we are right. False information shared with conviction does not help the truth!

 How do we react when Adventists are persecuted?

First of all, we try without delay to get the right information, which is not as easy as it sounds. This means finding out names, dates, and witnesses. If we have good correspondents, it works fast, but it is very difficult to get information. Perhaps the incident happened in an isolated place. Maybe members or witnesses are not well educated or are afraid to come forward because of threats. Rumors can spread fast in the world. Sometimes events happen in small towns or countries where our members are isolated. A news agency publishes the information and we have to act or react on that tenuous basis. Getting the full and correct information can take some time, which is why we have set a strategy.

It is necessary to work closely with the Communication Department of the General Conference. The Church has an organized network, and we need to use it effectively. The reaction has to be as fast as possible. A Church representative visits the location, meets with authorities and religious leaders—Adventists as well as non-Adventists—and gets the facts. At the same time, we contact international organizations, the United Nations Human Rights Commission, and non-governmental organizations that defend human rights and religious freedom. From our world headquarters, we visit the embassy of the country where the problem occurred and send letters to the government.

It must be an efficient, well-coordinated, and credible action, not based on rumors or inaccurate, partial information. The persecutors and the authorities that support them must know we are aware of the situation and will not abandon our brothers and sisters. It could be a long battle, but we must never give up. Governments must realize that persecuting a member of our Church is like persecuting the other 11 million Adventists. Sometimes we restrain ourselves so that we will not damage or cause problems for the work of our Church in the areas concerned. We cannot react without having the support of the local Adventist leaders and members. We do not implement our strategy, or parts of it, if our local and national church leaders disagree. In any case, we extend our help, are ready to visit the places and people, and will work until we succeed. We cannot do less.

 Is persecution a good thing?

Of course not. Persecution is evil and satanic in nature. We serve a God of love and freedom. He accepts homage only when it is freely given.

Jesus does make an interesting statement in the Beatitudes of the Sermon on the Mount, overlooking the Sea of Galilee: "Blessed are you when people insult you, persecute you . . ." (Matthew 5:11, NIV). Was Christ advocating persecution? Did *He* persecute or ask His followers to do so? Again, of course not, though it is the open scandal of historical Christianity that so-called Christians have persecuted and even killed.

One of the most blatant "Christian" crimes was the French Catholic army commander Simon de Montfort's leading his forces against "heretics." When he asked how his soldiers were to distinguish among the local civilian population between Catholics and heretics who had taken refuge in the Beziers church, it is reported the papal legate said, "Kill them all, God will know who are His own!" Yes, persecution is not so much evil because it is cruel, but it is cruel because it is both evil and blind.

Jesus did not say that persecution is blessed, but that His followers are blessed when suffering persecution. Why? Because persecution can be a badge of religious genuineness. It distinguishes the jellyfish from the resolute believer. Secondly, the persecuted person may develop deeper piety, faith in God, and purity (see *Testimonies*, Vol. 9, p. 228). Persecution can also promote unity and restoration of backsliders. But we should not speculate regarding persecution to wake the Church, but thank God for the freedom we have and live our faith and witness to the fullest.

Finally, the separating and scattering effect of persecution, imprisonment, and exile can contribute to the spread of the gospel. This was true in Paul's day, as was the case in Russia a hundred or so years ago, and in Sri Lanka as we write. Paul rejoiced because the gospel was spreading as a result of his imprisonment. Many others have experienced the same blessing.

All this does not mean that we should either call for or in any way condone persecution, for it is intrinsically evil. On the contrary, we must do our best to restrain it, knowing that like an illness it can come suddenly. Some people suffering from a confused persecution complex, expose themselves unnecessarily, and even invite persecution; Christ did not do so. A lot of false rumors about impending persecution or Sunday laws have circulated. Jesus warned against unhealthy worry about future events, and said, "Each day has enough trouble of its own" (Matthew 6:34, NIV), without transferring into the present the eschatological problems of the future.

We must oppose persecution for the sake of the truth and for the sake of evangelism to finish the work. The promise of the Beatitudes is that there is now to be blessedness, that is happiness, and a mighty flood of happiness to come, for the reward is great in heaven.

 Why have some western European governments published a list of "dangerous" sects?

Europe has historically had a problem with accepting religious freedom. Freedom is founded on much conflict and suffering. It took centuries before religious freedom was accepted, and it has not been easy to consistently respect it. The French Revolution is a good example. It was a violent answer to centuries of intolerance, religious wars, despotism, and inquisition. The year 1789 provided a strong breeze of freedom, including religious freedom, in which the Protestants played an important role. A few years later came a whirlwind producing terror and thousands and thousands of people were executed. Why? They were accused of being either real or potential enemies of freedom. It was a new inquisition on behalf of freedom. The persecuted became the persecutors, and the Catholic Church received a deadly wound. There were reasons for intolerance, but nevertheless, intolerance itself triumphed.

Publishing an official list of sects that are potentially "dangerous" comes from the same spirit of intolerance. On such a list, 172 religious associations or churches were listed in France, with 189 listed in Belgium! What are the criteria for a group to be listed as a "sect"? It is a mystery, because no real experts were contacted. This practice was denounced at Vienna during the 1999 meeting of the Organization for Security and Cooperation in Europe (OSCE), in the United Nations Commission on Human Rights, and by the United States Department of State. Now in France, there is an "Inter-Ministerial Mission to Combat Sects." Laws are voted, and the media are amplifying this hostility. How, in the area of religious liberty, can it be that countries like France and Belgium, which are so eager to preach human rights, are so blind concerning their own discrimination? Such lists feed intolerance and exclusion. Have they forgotten Article 18 of the United Nation's Universal Declaration of Human Rights? No, but they want to exclude certain churches and religious groups from this right. They have a selective and discriminatory understanding of religious freedom. Freedom is only for those who are approved or recognized by the authorities.

Unfortunately, the general population does not react against this dangerous trend. France and Belgium are very secularized, though the traditional religion is Roman Catholicism. After Waco, the mass suicide of the Solar Temple, and other tragedies, people are suspicious or even afraid of cults. Strong propaganda distributed by the establishment creates the feeling that religious minorities are dangerous or at least potentially dangerous. Fortunately, experts and scholars have reacted, though they were criticized and accused of being paid by the Scientologists or Jehovah's Witnesses to speak up for religious freedom. However, the courts have, on several occasions, reacted to this manipulation. Scientologists were recognized as a religion, which was a strong refutation of government policy. We have to pay tribute to those who serve and strengthen freedom and justice. France has always produced strong opponents to intolerance in its history. The anti-religious or anti-religious-minorities movements know that if they go too far, people will react on behalf of religious freedom.

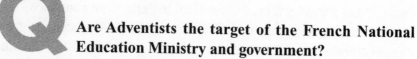

Are Adventists the target of the French National Education Ministry and government?

No, I would not say that. Adventists are indirect victims of anti-religious militancy among some fragments of the population and government officials. This faction cannot directly attack the traditional churches or religions, so they attack religious minorities in an attempt to get the support of the population. Their aim is to show that religion is an anachronism and leads people to the Dark Ages. While I was visiting two secondary schools in Martinique, French Antilles, the director of the first said, "There is no place here for those who do not attend classes on Saturday. We don't want to negotiate or to justify our position. It is a principle." I am sure that this man was theoretically in favor of human rights, and was against discrimination. But for him, religion was probably seen as having dangerous aspects (such as not sending your children to school on Saturday!), and it was his way of fighting ignorance and superstition. What concerns us is that people can be educated in the value of human rights in general, and nevertheless discriminate against people based on their religion. The enormous contradiction does not enter their minds.

The director of the second school had an opposite attitude. He welcomed us and made a clear statement: "The SDA students are welcome here, and we will always do our best to help them." He was of the Catholic faith. He gave hope! While you have fanatics on the one hand who deny some human rights, you have those who firmly defend them. You never know who will defend your rights. Defenders can be agnostics, humanists, ecumenists, Catholics, Protestants and others, but they all are in God's hands to defend and protect His people. While doing university studies in France, Adventist students in past decades almost always found help and understanding. Now it seems to be more difficult. We are working on finding solutions.

 Are Sabbath keepers in trouble in Western Europe?

Unfortunately, yes! Not everywhere, but there are problems in several countries that claim to defend human rights. In France there is a current anti-cult/sect obsession, and Adventist students and teachers can have serious problems. A few families lost their government family allowances because they would not send their children to public schools on Saturday.

In the past, Adventists found teachers or school principals open to their problem, and solutions were found in most cases. Hostility was rare. Now, in an anti-religious-minorities climate, a spirit of hostility is no longer a rare exception. Children are under pressure or humiliated, and their parents are sometimes publicly scorned—things that seemed to belong to history. Intolerance is growing. Several students have had to change schools in order to avoid losing a year of schooling. Fortunately, not all college and university teachers and secondary principals are anti-religious, and many are willing to make helpful arrangements.

On the other hand, in several other European countries the Sabbath problem has been dealt with positively for Seventh-day Adventists. In some countries there are specific laws recognizing the rights of Seventh-day Adventists to observe the Sabbath—in public employment, in schools, and even in the military.

 Why are some Islamic countries so against religious freedom?

Probably because they see Islam as having or being the truth and view all other religions as in error. Error, they think, should have no rights and should be excised like a malignant cancer, or at least should be contained and not be permitted to spread. This mind-set reminds us of the medieval church, which stamped out heresy using the secular arm. Catholicism of the nineteenth century still upheld the Inquisition, albeit in attenuated forms, and proclaimed the *Syllabus of Errors*, which included forms of religious liberty characterized as ravings of demented minds. Indeed, the Christian record regarding religious liberty is abysmal.

The liberals in Muslim countries accept the right of Christians to worship freely, but even the liberals generally do not accept the right of Christians to practice their religion by engaging in evangelism among Muslims. Muslim extremists will not even allow one Christian church to function in Saudi Arabia, despite the presence of perhaps half a million or so Christians working in that country. The far-fetched explanation advanced is that all of Saudi Arabia is a religious "mosque" and the country so holy it cannot tolerate other worship within its borders. All this repudiates the practice of the Prophet Muhammad and the teaching of the Koran that there is to be "no constraint in religion."

Muslims generally do not accept the basic human right to *change* one's religion. To be more precise, they claim a Muslim does not have or need this right, because he already has the true religion! Again, we have here the medieval concept that error has no rights. Of course, all this is in glaring contradiction to the international human rights and religious-liberty instruments. Though we are faced with a sort of Islamic fundamentalist religious "iron curtain," let us remember that we serve a mighty God of liberty, whose plans know no haste and no delay. Even the Berlin Wall came tumbling down, despite being buttressed by a powerful and well-organized police state. Someday the Islamic "cordon sanitaire" will break.

 Did our Church in Romania sue the government in 1999?

Actually, our Church did not sue the government. Let us explain what happened and praise the Lord for what He did! Our Church is fully recognized in Romania, where we have more than 85,000 baptized members. This means that every Saturday, more than 100,000 adults and children attend church. In 1998, the Romanian Ministry of National Education decided to give, on a Saturday in 1999, the third and final part of their national secondary school test. The Church and the Romanian Religious Liberty Association reacted and intervened, asking for a change in the date. The government in Romania replied that this year it was not possible to change the test date. The Saturday test date affected about 1,000 Adventist students.

In Bucharest, several parents decided to take the issue to court, and they lost! The test was held on Saturday, June 5, 1999. Approximately 640 Adventist students did not take the test. The authorities were surprised by the number of students who refused to take the test on Saturday, thereby forfeiting one year of school work. They were impressed that the students would not transgress their consciences. The parents went to the Supreme Court in Bucharest, and they won!

The Ministry of National Education was handed an order to organize another test before July 30. They had about 20 days to do that. Of course, the decision of the court was contested and other difficulties arose, but finally the government set a date for the Adventist students. It was very significant that for the first time, the Adventists in Romania decided to publicly defend their rights. The apostle Paul did the same. Several times he said to the police or to the magistrate: "I am a Roman citizen!" The law is there to defend honest and good citizens.

 Have churches published commitments to religious liberty?

Yes, they have! Here is a short sampling (there are many others):

1. Catholic Church: "Declaration on Religious Freedom: Dignitatis Humanae" (December 7, 1965, adopted by the Second Vatican Council). In its conclusion, the document states " . . . it is necessary that religious freedom be everywhere provided with an effective constitutional guarantee and that respect be shown for the high duty and right of man freely to lead his religious life in society."

2. World Council of Churches: "Declaration on Religious Liberty," adopted at the First Assembly of the WCC in Amsterdam in 1948. On p. 69 we read, "The rights of religious freedom herein declared shall be recognized and observed for all persons without distinctions as race, color, sex, language, or religion, and without imposition of disabilities by virtue of legal provision of administrative acts" (*Religion and Human Rights: Basic Documents*; edited by Tod Stahnke and J. Paul Martin, Columbia University, 1998, p. 207).

3. Baptist World Alliance: "Manifesto on Religious Freedom,"

adopted at the Seventh Baptist World Congress, Copenhagen, August 1947. "It is our first duty to extend the rights of conscience to all people, irrespective of their race, color, sex, or religion (or lack of religion)" (ibid., p. 205).

4. The Seventh-day Adventist "Statement on Religious Freedom," voted at the General Conference Session, Utrecht, The Netherlands, July 8, 1995. In the first paragraph we read, "For more than a century, Seventh-day Adventists have been active promoters of religious freedom." *The Seventh-day Adventist Encyclopedia* also has an article on "Religious Liberty." There is also the following statement: "Bigoted and intolerant religious extremism, of whatever type, must be deplored and halted. Every person has the right to express his or her religious ideas with conviction, but always with respect for the rights of others" (*Statements, Guidelines, and Other Documents*, General Conference of Seventh-day Adventists, 1996, p. 46).

Q **Are international human rights instruments relevant enough to help provide religious freedom?**

Yes, they are. A problem arises when they are not implemented. What happens when this is the case? This is the big question! For example, Iran can persecute the Baha'i and Sudan the Christians. Do such countries have real problems as a result? Have the Western or other countries, which signed and support these instruments, stopped their relations with countries that have no religious freedom? In the United Nations, are the member countries that have violated human rights and religious freedom ostracized or penalized? Of course they are mentioned as deficient and their image is tarnished, but is that enough? In spite of all this, the texts exist, and those countries that ignore them have the burden to explain why they do so.

There are four categories of international instruments:

1. Treaties
2. Declarations
3. Authoritative interpretations of treaties
4. Reciprocal political commitments

1. Treaties

The benchmark is the 1966 International Covenant on Civil and Political Rights (ICCPR). Most of the states in the world, including the United States, have ratified the covenant and thus are obligated to implement it. In addition, there are regional treaties like the European Convention on Human Rights, American Convention on Human Rights, and the African Charter of Human and Peoples' Rights. The UNESCO Convention Against Discrimination in Education is especially interesting for us. Article 1 may be applied to Sabbath problems. Article 5 concerns the role and authority of parents. The Convention on the Rights of the Child (Articles 1 and 14) reinforces the UNESCO Convention on Discrimination in Education.

2. Declarations

Declarations are not ratified by the states, but they constitute a "customary international law." The United Nations Universal Declaration of Human Rights is, of course, the most known and respected declaration. But do not forget the "Declaration on the Elimination of All Forms of Intolerance and Discrimination Based on Religion or Belief." It was adopted unanimously, that is, without a vote, on November 25, 1981. Article 6, Section (h) includes the right to observe a day of rest according to the precept of one's religion. Adventists, especially Dr. Gianfranco Rossi, made here a significant contribution.

3. Authoritative interpretations of treaties

There are official comments on the texts. The United Nations Human Rights Committee issued a very important document on article 18 of the ICCPR. In *General Comments* #22 (48), item 1, we read: "The fundamental character of these freedoms (thought, conscience, and religion) is also reflected in the fact that this provision cannot be derogated from, even in time of public emergency, as stated in Article 4(2) of the Covenant" (*Religion and Human Rights: Basic Documents*, Columbia University, 1998, p 92). This same committee has also stated that the right to have a "religion of one's choice" implies the right to change one's religion.

4. Reciprocal political commitments

The Organization for Security and Cooperation in Europe (OSCE) exhibits a most significant political commitment in the area of religious liberty and human rights. Article 16 of the 1989 concluding document of Vienna concerns religious freedom. The United States is a member of the OSCE with 53 other countries. Freedom of religion is also mentioned in many other official texts. We are not without support to defend this great and essential principle.

The Cairo Declaration on Human Rights in Islam, adopted and issued at the Nineteenth Islamic Conference of Foreign Ministers in Cairo on August 5, 1990, has its own particular way to introduce religious freedom. Article 10 is interesting to read: "Islam is the religion of unspoiled nature. It is prohibited to exercise any form of compulsion on man or to exploit his poverty or ignorance in order to convert him to another religion or to atheism" (Ibid., p. 87).

 What does the *Religious Freedom World Report 1999* teach us?

The *World Report*, published in March 1999 by the General Conference Department of Public Affairs and Religious Liberty states that there is increasing religious persecution in the world. As Adventists, we need to be aware of religious groups that are the special target of persecution, for we, too, can become victims of intolerance. Intolerance, like a malignant cancer, tends to spread and attack other healthy organs.

Many Christian churches have been destroyed or burned in Indonesia. Our people may believe that because we have had no church burned there, we do not need to be concerned. If people, Christian or not, are persecuted for their beliefs, we need to express solidarity and try to help; our time may also come.

In the *World Report,* six countries are listed as being in "Category 5," which means that there is no religious freedom at all in those countries and that we have no churches there. These countries are Afghanistan, Brunei, Libya, Mauritania, Saudi Arabia, and Syria. This does not mean that we have no Adventists at all in these countries, but that our Church, as an organization, cannot exist. Syria is a special case and should not be listed in this category, but our Church was expelled from there several decades ago at the time of the war between Syria and Israel. We believe that things are, gradually, taking a turn for the better. Some promising contacts have recently been made.

Thirty-nine countries are listed in "Category 3" and "Category 4," which means that there have been, in those countries, serious difficulties and violations against religious freedom. Some countries listed in "Category 2" are on the edge of "Category 3." We will see next year how things evolve.

The yearly *World Report* will become an essential contribution of our Church for human rights investigations. A few weeks after the *Report* was first published, the United Nations Special Rapporteur on Religious Intolerance requested additional information on several cases. The United States Department of State did the same concerning Uzbekistan. Our ambition is to become a reliable source of information concerning especially Adventists who experience serious intolerance or are persecuted for their faith, no matter where.

How can the *Religious Freedom World Report 1999* help the persecuted member?

Every year the United Nations Special Rapporteur on Religious Intolerance (violations of freedom of religion and belief) gives a report in Geneva at the Plenary Session of the Human Rights Commission. Most of the governments of the world are represented at this meeting. In harmony with the provisions of the 1981 "Declaration on the Elimination of All Forms of Intolerance and Discrimination Based on Religion or Belief," those governments or countries accused of violating religious freedom are expected to give an explanation. No government wants to see its country listed negatively in the report of the Special Rapporteur, as it is not good for their image. During this plenary session, the recognized Non-Governmental Organizations (NGOs) have five minutes each to speak on the various items of the agenda. The General Conference is recognized as an NGO, Category II. Every year we can exercise our right to speak. Some Adventists are also speakers for other NGOs.

A country cited for its lack of religious freedom is expected to receive a visit from the Special Rapporteur for an investigation. If they refuse, they lose face. If they accept, they have to allow for an investigation. Because of the "sect" issue, Germany was investigated. Other countries like Sudan, the United States, and Vietnam were investigated, and the report was introduced in the Plenary Session.

The information we publish in the *World Report* can be quoted and verified by the United Nations. Also, the United States Department of State and the Office of Religious Freedom Abroad issue similar reports on a yearly basis. The countries that are listed need to explain intolerance and why they persecute believers. For example, July 22, 1997, the "Bureau of Democracy, Human Rights, and Labor Affairs" published a report on religious freedom focusing on Christians. Countries are listed with: "Current situation" and "U.S. Government Action." On February 26, 1999, the U.S. Department of State published a report on France focusing on the anti-sect policy of the French government. You can also find many reports from Amnesty International. Most governments involved are unhappy with this kind of negative publicity. I believe that our *World Report* helped our members who were in prison in Cape Verde and in Sri Lanka. A country like Saudi Arabia is constantly attacked for the total absence of religious freedom. Their answers to the UN Special Rapporteur tend to discredit them in this regard. Hopefully, a change will come one day.

 Why did the United States in 1998 vote the International Religious Freedom Act (IRFA)?

To simplify, it is the United States' answer to the increasing religious persecution in the world. For the first time in its history, the U.S. voted a law to protect and defend religious freedom abroad. This is remarkable and unique. The law came as the result of strong pressure on the government from the Evangelical Christians. The issue was first introduced by members of the Christian Coalition and then received the support of many Christians. From reports and news, it appears that Christians are being persecuted in more and more countries, especially in Islamic countries. Most of these countries have been receiving U.S. aid from public taxes, and taxpayers ask, "What is our government doing to protect our brothers and sisters in Christ?"

To defend Christians in the world is not currently a priority of governments. How many governments have denounced Sudan, Saudi Arabia, Iran, Egypt, and Vietnam for the persecution of Christians? The non-western Christians are alone, and as a minority in several countries, they can be oppressed and persecuted. Their countrymen accuse them of being spies from the West and the U.S. because they have the "wrong" religion. What has been happening for years in some parts of the world, is a form of religious cleansing. You are a

Christian? Go to America! A few years from now, how many Christians will be living in the Middle East? In Pakistan? In Iran? In Lebanon? This is just to mention a few countries.

In the United States, Christians are becoming more and more sensitive to persecution. They say, "We don't want our tax money supporting governments that persecute fellow Christians." President Clinton opened a door by establishing the "U.S. Advisory Committee on Religious Persecution Abroad." We were invited several times to attend its meetings. Several bills were introduced in Congress. One became law after being signed by the president: "The International Religious Freedom Act" (IRFA). The Presbyterians played an important part in drafting this Act. This law gives a strong message from the United States of America to the world, especially those countries that deny individuals religious freedom. This demonstrates that the most powerful country in the world stands for religious freedom, not only for Protestants, Catholics, and traditional religions, but for all religions. The U.S. government stands for the principle of religious freedom, which is a core value of American society. Religious persecution is integrated in the human rights report of the U.S. Department of State. Even U.S. allies such as Germany, France, and Austria have been taken to task for lapses in religious liberty. This is a new day.

Will the IRFA justify military intervention by the U.S.? No! There are several steps to be taken in response to persecution. It is not an aggressive process, but it is a dissuasive one. It is good to encourage governments to think about the rights of religious minorities. No government wants to be pointed out as a bad example and perhaps risk trade sanctions, especially when the country that is doing the pointing is the world's superpower!

What does the International Religious Freedom Act (IRFA) state?

If you read the "Final Report of the Advisory Committee on Religious Freedom Abroad to the Secretary of State and to the President of the United States" published May 17, 1999, you will have all the answers you need. The IRFA is the concrete result of the work of 20 religious leaders and experts who have been working together for two years on religious freedom abroad. This new law "provides the U.S. government with a renewed mandate and appropriate mechanisms to promote religious freedom as an integral part of U.S. foreign policy" (p. 89). *There is no other government in the world so committed to religious freedom,* and we must underline this fact. The approach is moderate, and the IRFA does not "mandate automatic sanctions . . . nor does it favor any particular faith or discrimination against any other."

Three new institutions were created:

1. An Office for International Religious Freedom in the Department of State, headed by an Ambassador-at-large;
2. A quasi-independent Commission on International Religious Freedom;
3. A special advisor to the U.S. National Security Council.

The law also requires an annual report to be issued by the Office for International Religious Freedom. It is important to bring religious freedom back to the human rights agenda, for religious freedom is the basic human right.

Are the IRFA and the International Court of Justice "signs of the times"?

We are tempted to say they are good signs. People appear eager to support justice and to defend victims, but the IRFA and the Court are two different things. Actually, the United States voted against the final action establishing the International Court of Justice. Before the meeting in Naples, Italy, we received a briefing by the U.S. Ambassador for Religious Freedom. He explained to our group of human-rights advocates the importance and the necessity of this international court. Its purpose is to have arrested and to judge "war criminals." Except for the Nuremberg Tribunal and the courts for Bosnia and Rwanda, there is no international court to judge war criminals. This means that a person can kill thousands of innocent people and spend the rest of his or her life in luxury, out of reach in a country that will offer protection. With an International Court of Justice, this will be more difficult to arrange. War criminals will be judged, and the countries that protect them will have sanctions placed on them. This International Court is not to be used to persecute people, but to protect them.

The International Religious Freedom Act is an American law, a unique law in the world. Its purpose is to restrain religious persecution. Although the IRFA and the proposed court are different entities, both have a global dimension. They are a sign of globalization and of the need to protect people anywhere and everywhere.

Adventists and Other Churches

 What is the ecumenical movement?

First, a little bit of humor: "Ecumenical" has nothing to do with "economical," though some people at times confuse the two terms! It is a Greek word referring to the entire inhabited earth. Synonyms would be universal or catholic. The ecumenical movement is an activity that gained increasing momentum among Christians during the twentieth century. It aims at regaining or achieving some form of worldwide Christian unity across denominational barriers. It reached its organizational peak in 1948, when the World Council of Churches was organized, and its emotive high around 1968, soon after the Second Vatican Council, when the Catholic Church climbed aboard the ecumenical boat; originally, the Catholic Church was much opposed.

During the first half or two-thirds of the twentieth century, the emphasis among many ecumenists was to achieve some form of *organic* unity; some even grew lyrical and dreamed about having "one church." Much emphasis was on church mergers, united churches, multilateral dialogs, and Eucharistic fellowship.

The ecumenical movement consisted of three main streams, Faith and Order (theology), Life and Work (practical, socioeconomic Christianity) and the International Missionary Council (foreign missionary work). By 1961 the last of these three streams had merged into the World Council of Churches (WCC). While the WCC should not be seen as tantamount to the ecumenical movement, which is much broader, it is its major organizational manifestation. Many convinced ecumenists would go further and say the WCC is the movement's "privileged instrument."

There is a wealth of other ecumenical organizations, many cooperating or "in association" with the WCC. There are scores of national or regional councils—such as the National Council of Churches in the USA or the European Conference of Churches. Numerous ecumenical institutes have been established, and quite a number of churches have offices for ecumenical affairs.

Many churches, especially the old-line churches, clearly affirm their support of the ecumenical movement. Not a few churches, while belonging to the WCC, really only give lip service to ecumenism and certainly make no financial contribution. Other churches are members but seem to form the ecumenical equivalent of "Her Majesty's Loyal Opposition" in the Westminster Parliament!

There are churches that are openly and vociferously opposed to anything associated with ecumenism. They can get quite rabid in their attacks and see the ecumenical movement as the major bane of church life today. Still others, like the Seventh-day Adventist Church, have, out of concern for truth and the prophetic mission, kept their distance, not sailing on the ecumenical boat, but acknowledging some of the positive achievements, such as religious liberty, less hostile interchurch relations, and greater justice in human relations. Thus, while not writing off the ecumenical movement, Adventism has been openly critical of various aspects.

Is there just *one* ecumenical movement?

A frequently heard unity slogan in World Council of Churches circles is "there is only one ecumenical movement." While it is understandable why ecumen-thusiasts trumpet this catch phrase, it represents much more a desire than a credible reality. The facts are that at the end of the twentieth century, which has been called the "ecumenical century," there are various approaches to ecumenism that inevitably produce in actuality different ecumenical movements.

It is quite easy to understand that staunch—even professional—advocates of Christian unity like to think in terms of *one* unity movement, because *several* movements does not sound nearly as successful and united. However, the very fact that some ecumenists keep on talking about "one movement," reveals that they see there is a problem of plurality to be confronted or at least avoided.

Both Roman Catholicism and Orthodoxy have their own more monocentric approaches to ecumenism. The Orthodox Churches are currently rather unhappy within the World Council of Churches, feeling slighted and dominated by liberal Protestant churches. They affirm their support of the unity movement, but increasingly they are at loggerheads with mainstream WCC ecumenism, and threaten to suspend WCC membership; some Orthodox bodies already have.

The Catholic Church at the Second Vatican Council (1964) climbed aboard the ecumenical boat, but has not joined the World Council of Churches. By its very nature, Catholicism thinks in terms of "one ecumenical movement," but that is a future goal to be reached, with the pope being assigned the central office and symbol of unity and discernment of truth. At the Second Vatican Council, Rome rejected in its *Decree on Ecumenism* the wording "Principles of *Catholic Ecumenism*" in favor of *"Catholic Principles* of Ecumenism." Nevertheless, Rome has continued to march down its own unity road, without deviating much toward Geneva, Constantinople, or Canterbury. It will become an integral part of the "one ecumenical movement" on its own terms and when the time is right.

The World Evangelical Fellowship is an important unity and cooperative movement bringing together scores of millions of evangelicals from all parts of the world. The Pentecostal experience is another powerful uniting movement, touching several hundred million lives. Both these movements listen to a different ecumenical drummer (the musical score often even sounds anti-ecumenical!).

Seventh-day Adventists see themselves as a worldwide—therefore "ecumenical"—unity movement in over 200 nations, calling for biblical, doctrinal, and Christ-centered unity—"pressing together"—in preparation for the soon-coming Lord, and the establishment of His universal kingdom, the world (that is the true *oikumene*) to come (see Hebrews 6:5).

 We understand the Seventh-day Adventist Church is considered to be a Christian World Communion (CWC). Is this correct?

Basically, the Christian World Communions are the recognized Christian world bodies. There are, however, considerable differences between these CWCs. Most of them are umbrella organizations for churches that belong to the same confession or communion, such as the Baptist World Alliance, the World Methodist Council, or the Lutheran World Federation. Other Christian World Communions are really world churches, such as the Seventh-day Adventist Church, the Salvation Army, the Roman Catholic Church, and the Ecumenical Patriarchate of Constantinople.

Most denominations are organized as national churches and therefore find it helpful to have international coordinating bodies. For example, the Anglican Consultative Council helps bring Anglicans, such as the Church of England and U.S. Episcopal Church, into closer solidarity, cooperation, and communion. There are about twenty such bodies, and they meet together in an informal conference of secretaries once a year, usually in October. About half the meetings take place in Switzerland; the other meetings are held in other locations, mostly in Europe (for logistic and financial reasons). The conference is a forum for exchange of information, and consideration of international religious issues, such as religious liberty, interchurch relations, and bilateral dialogs. It is a unique opportunity for Christian fellowship, but not a decision-making conference.

 Are the Christian World Communions part of the ecumenical movement?

One can look at this question in various ways. The term *ecumenism* has many different meanings. If we mean by ecumenism increased religious understanding and cooperation across national borders, then the CWCs can be seen as ecumenical, some bringing unity to their confessional family by coordinating, across national borders, the work of their member denominations.

Some CWCs are supportive of the organized movement for Christian unity as epitomized by the World Council of Churches. After all, Presbyterians, Anglicans, and Lutherans were very much involved in founding and leading out in the WCC. After originally being opposed to the ecumenical movement, the Roman Catholic Church now officially stands for Christian unity—of course, largely on its terms. The two Orthodox CWCs (Constantinople and Moscow Patriarchates) have recently adopted a very critical attitude toward the WCC, even hinting at possibly leaving the WCC.

Other CWCs, such as the Seventh-day Adventist Church, World Evangelical Fellowship, and Baptist World Alliance have expressed for many years serious reservations regarding various aspects of ecumenism, and their churches are generally not members of the WCC. Some of these churches could be said to exhibit anti-ecumenical views.

Why do Adventists not believe in unity?

This question is very much like the question "Have you stopped beating your wife?" It is really a misleading question that sets up a falsehood, and thus sends people on the wrong scent.

The fact is, Adventists believe in worldwide Christian unity. There are very few world churches, most churches being nationally organized and administered. The General Conference is the body that administratively holds the world Church together. There is one *Church Manual*, from Iceland to Japan, and in the more than 200 countries where the Church lives and operates. There is one set of 27 fundamental beliefs, and Sabbath School lessons are very similar in all parts of the world. How could we be opposed to unity, when our Lord Himself prayed for the unity of the church modeled after the unity between God the Father and God the Son (see John 17). We believe in one Lord, one faith, one baptism.

When you read Christ's high priestly prayer in John 17, it becomes clear that the unity He prayed for is not just any unity, based on conflicting doctrines coated over with some form of mutual recognition, but a unity in *truth*, in *love*, in *evangelism*, and *personal sanctification*. When one of these elements is absent, authentic unity is missing; that is the Seventh-day Adventist position.

Perhaps we need to make better known our passionate belief and search for unity across geographical, ideological, ethnic, and gender borders. Indeed, we have been told to "press together, press together" (*Selected Messages*, book 2, p. 374). Let us continue to do so more than ever, for there are many centrifugal forces trying to pull the Church apart. Under God, the gravity of the gospel and prophetic mass holding the church of the remnant together will overcome the forces of division.

Is the Seventh-day Adventist Church a member of the World Council of Churches?

The answer is a clear no. We have never been members, we are not now, and we have no plans to become members of the WCC as it has been organized for the past half-century.

Unfortunately, some dishonest or at best badly misinformed individuals have circulated false information to the effect that we are members. Not only are we not full members, but we are not even partial members, though in truth, such a category does not exist.

We pay no dues or funds to the WCC and, not being members, we have no voting rights and can send no delegates to its assemblies, central committee or commission meetings. It should be pointed out that only churches can belong to the WCC; councils of churches cannot. Thus, it is false to claim that the Seventh-day Adventist Church is a member of the WCC, because in a few cases the SDA Church has some relationship (e.g. observer status) with a national council of churches in a given country.

It is also wrong and misleading to say the SDA Church is a member of the WCC because an Adventist may be a member of one of its commissions. True, for some years a distinguished SDA theologian was in his own personal capacity elected by the WCC as a member of its Faith and Order Commission, but this did not make the SDA Church a member. This arrangement did provide the Church with helpful insights, in addition to acquainting some of the world's leading theologians with a well-articulated Adventist viewpoint.

 Why is the Seventh-day Adventist Church not a member of the World Council of Churches?

The quick and superficial answer is that we have not been invited to join, nor have we applied for membership. It is likely that if the SDA Church applied for membership she would be eligible to join, though there might be objections from some unenlightened member churches. These few falsely claim that Adventists do not believe in the Trinity (which is a key doctrinal basis of the WCC) and accuse Adventists in certain countries of disturbing the religious peace by engaging in unbecoming proselytism.

We acknowledge up front that the WCC has some laudable aims and has achieved or stood for several positive things. No Adventist can be opposed to the unity Christ Himself prayed for. The WCC has opposed diatribe and harsh interchurch relations; it has helped remove unfounded prejudices. It has helped provide more accurate information on churches and has strongly promoted human rights, including religious liberty. It has combated the evils of racism, and not just when this became politically correct. It has drawn attention to socioeconomic implications of the gospel.

From a Seventh-day Adventist perspective there are several obstacles to membership. The main problem is Adventist prophetic understanding. We believe, hopefully without pride or arrogance, that this Church represents the divinely appointed key instrument for the organized proclamation of the eternal gospel discerned from the prophetic vantage point of Revelation 14 and 18. Seventh-day Adventists see themselves as the "historical remnant" gathering the "faithful remnant" out of religious opposition to the purposes of God. The ethos is thus markedly different from the ecumenical call to inclusive unity of quite separate and divergent, even conflicting, elements.

There are other problems upon which we can touch only very succinctly. Much ecumenical understanding of Scripture does not see the Bible as a unity, normative and authoritative in itself. The WCC tends to downplay evangelism and personal sanctification and revival. The emphasis is on social morality and "converting" the unjust structures of society. A laudable goal, but this is not biblical conversion.

Apostasy and heresy are terms with a long Christian tradition, but they are almost systematically avoided in ecumenical circles. This is understandable, because they do not fit very comfortably into the ecumenical picture and the hoped-for unity of all humankind. Some ecumenists give the impression (hopefully just an impression) that there are only three heresies: (1) disunity; (2) anti-Trinitarianism; and (3) racism. However, the New Testament shows the threat of anti-Christian penetration within "the temple of God" itself (2 Thessalonians 2:3, 4). The eschatological picture of the church at the end of the great controversy between good and evil, between Christ and Satan, is not of a megachurch gathering all humankind around the great white throne, but of a remnant faithful to God and His commandments (see Revelation 12:17).

 Do Adventists at times participate in meetings of the WCC or other ecumenical bodies?

The answer is yes, but this needs to be qualified and explained. We are invited from time to time (perhaps on the average once a year) to send "observers" (or equivalent) to assemblies or some other conferences of the WCC. Since the WCC, as do other Christian World Communions, recognizes the General Conference of Seventh-day Adventists as a Christian World Communion, it invites the General Conference to send an "advisor" to meetings of the Central Committee. These non-delegate categories provide us the opportunity to keep informed regarding plans and developments and make our viewpoint known in a polite but honest way. They also help us to become acquainted with and even make friends with some of the top religious leaders in the world. As a result, Adventists on the international level are now increasingly respected as members of a significant church that needs to be taken seriously, and not viewed as an isolationist and heretical sect. Much progress has been made, though we still have work to do.

Are the Evangelicals warming up to the Roman Catholic Church?

It is very clear that doctrinally most so-called Conservative Evangelicals have been quite far away from Roman Catholics; *this is still the case.* In the past, relations between these wings of Christianity were strained, each having quite a few pointed, not to say hostile, things to say about the other. The fact that in Latin America millions of people, at least formally members of the Catholic Church, have left Catholicism in favor of Evangelicalism (Baptists, Pentecostals and others) has further antagonized relations.

In 1994 a number of Roman Catholic and Evangelical theologians, some of them well known, produced a joint statement called "Evangelicals and Catholics Together: The Christian Mission in the Third Millennium." Some watchers of the ecumenical scene have heralded this event as signifying that Evangelicals and Catholics are now coming together, reaching across the doctrinal abyss, and that broad-based theological agreements could soon be reached. While the Joint Statement has some practical significance, it is blowing things out of proportion to talk about Evangelical-Catholic unity being just around the theological corner.

First of all, the Joint Statement was a relatively small private venture, individuals signing on in their personal capacity, in no way committing their churches. In fact, several Evangelical church leaders were unhappy with the signing of such a document, disavowed it, and some of the authors were taken to task for writing and signing it.

In reading the document, one soon realizes that the Statement is not announcing doctrinal agreement, but on the contrary makes it clear that there are major disagreements that cannot be papered over. The agreement is essentially limited to mission in the sociopolitical arena, and even there it centers largely on the issue of dealing with *abortion.* That is where there is agreement: a cooperative sociopolitical program to stop abortion and strengthen public morality in the weakened areas of marriage and the family. Cooperation regarding a political agenda is not Christian unity.

Evangelicals are far from accepting the papal system, the sacrifice of the mass, veneration of the Virgin Mary and certain saints, ministerial (priestly) celibacy, authority of tradition, indulgences and good works on behalf of the dead.

 What is the unity the World Council of Churches is aiming for at the turn of the millennium?

In the early and perhaps more utopian days of the ecumenical movement, the constant intention was to achieve organic unity in some form or another, aiming at a united church. As the decades passed, it became increasingly clear that this was an illusory goal, somewhat like chasing the golden ecumenical pot at the end of the theological rainbow. Every time some problem was solved and some organizational unity achieved, another problem and another split would occur. While some denominations were indeed drawing closer together, new divisions were taking place, causing intra-denominational tensions and dissensions.

Today, ecumenists seem to be rather more realistic and restrained. The pre-Vatican II euphoria has been replaced by more down-to-the-pew common sense. The current ecumenical goal is to reach what is labeled "visible unity." Unity and fellowship, yes, but across organizational and denominational lines, which would remain. Organic unity is increasingly out, and unity of fellowship is in.

The practical aim is to achieve *mutual recognition* by separate churches, acknowledging each other as belonging to the church of Christ, the Una Sancta. The key elements requiring mutual recognition are three: (1) Baptism; (2) Lord's Supper (Holy Communion or Eucharist); and (3) Ministry. In both baptism and Eucharist, the key problems are the sacramental understanding of their meaning. Acceptance of each other's ordained ministry involves the questions of laying on of hands in physical "apostolic succession" and historic episcopacy.

There is not the slightest chance that agreement across the board will soon be reached, to give "visible unity" a millennial send-off party! However, some significant steps have taken place in the late nineties, for example, between Anglicans (including Episcopalians) and Lutherans, and between Lutherans and Moravians.

 What is the consensus required by the Roman Catholic Church in order to establish visible Christian unity with other churches?

The Vatican does not go into all kinds of doctrinal details, outlining dozens of doctrines people and churches would have to believe in order to be in full communion with Rome and achieve visible unity. The Catholic Church currently indicates, as we understand it, that in order to achieve Christian unity between Rome and other churches there would need to be *consensus* (though probably not detail agreement on everything) regarding five matters:

1. Consensus would have to be reached in regard to the relationship between the Bible and tradition. There is certainly nothing new here.
2. Consensus regarding the triple significance of the Lord's Supper as memorial, sacrifice, and real presence of Christ. Again nothing new.
3. Some form of agreement regarding the three-fold ministerial ordination (deacon, priest, bishop) in apostolic succession. No surprise.
4. Consensus regarding the *magisterium* or teaching authority of the church, including the role of the pope and that of the bishops, individually and as a college. This comes from Vatican II.

5. Consensus regarding the role of the Virgin Mary, as mother and intercessor with Christ. Here we detect the handiwork of the Polish pope.

All this sounds rather simple and straightforward, but complicated issues and deep divides are found within these five points. Let us not hold our breath until consensus is reached on these issues between Catholics and Protestants. True, there has been quite a reaching of hands across the gulf of separation, but the abyss is still very wide and deep.

 Are Ellen G. White's writings an obstacle to interchurch relations?

It depends on the text we read, the context, and our own presuppositions. When Ellen White wrote about the end of time, which is a small part of her writings, she portrayed the official churches as opposed to religious freedom and to the faithful remnant. However, she always made a clear distinction between systems, organizations, and sincere members. We are not saved because we are "Protestants," "Catholics," or "Adventists." We are saved because Jesus died for us. We should never forget that the religious organizations will become part of "Babylon," when they will unite their power to persecute those who do not accept their creed. The apocalyptic definition of the "wicked" is linked to their acts. They are wrong and doing the devil's work, because they persecute those "who keep God's commandments and the faith of Jesus" (Revelation 14:12). In reading what Ellen G. White wrote about churches and religions, we should always take the context into account. Are we persecuted by the "Protestants"? Are we systematically persecuted by the Vatican today?

When the servant of the Lord wrote about Christian life and pastoral care, she favored good relations. She wrote: "Our ministers should seek to come near to the ministers of other denominations. Pray for and with these men, for whom Christ is interceding. A solemn responsibility is theirs. As Christ's messengers we should manifest a deep, earnest interest in these shepherds of the flock" (*Testimonies*, vol. 6, p. 78). This is not what we might call an "anti-relations" concept. This is not a strategy of isolating ourselves from others. She also wrote, "The Lord has His representatives in all the churches" (Ibid., p. 70).

She warned pastors and lay members who attack other churches: "Be cautious in your labors, brethren, not to assail the prejudices of the people too strongly. There should be no going out of the way to attack other denominations: for it only creates a combative spirit, and closes ears and hearts to the entrance of the truth. We have our work to do, which is not to tear down but to build up" (Manuscript Releases, vol. 20, 136.3).

We may continue to quote Ellen White, showing that her position was not in favor of isolation and aggressiveness towards other churches. She wrote, "The Lord has not given His people the work of making a tirade against those who are transgressing His law. In no case are we to make a raid on the other churches" (*Review and Herald,* April 20, 1911, par. 21). To say that Ellen White's writings are an obstacle to cultivating sincere and good relations with other believers is incorrect. We are not alone on earth, and we will not be alone in the new earth. Having good relations with others does not mean that we favor the current focus of ecumenism. We should have good relations with our neighbors, as I hope we have, but this does not mean that we are giving up our faith! It does not mean either that we want to force others to convert. If we love people in spite of our differences, our testimony will be strong.

Should Adventists meet with other ministers and have dialogue with Christian churches?

Certainly dialogue is better than diatribe. Isolation breeds ignorance and misunderstanding, and leads to insularity. You might be surprised by the false and ludicrous conceptions that circulate regarding Adventists. Just to mention a few:

1. Adventists are legalists and believe that Sabbath keeping or tithe paying will save them; Satan is their savior.
2. They do not believe in the divinity of Christ; they place the writings of a 19th century prophet above or at least as equal to the Scriptures.
3. They believe that only Adventists will be saved and that Christ is going to return on the seventh day.
4. Seventh-day Adventists have and continue to set dates for the second coming of Christ.
5. Adventists would rather die than eat meat.

These and other views are held and disseminated by non-Adventist Christians. Should we not do our best to set the record straight, both for our sake and theirs?

The apostle Peter charges us to always be ready to explain to others the reason for our hope and belief (see 1 Peter 3:15) Ellen G. White instructs our ministers to meet with other ministers. She asks us to "come near to ministers of other denominations." She not only instructs us to pray *for* them, but *with* them, and interestingly enough she calls them "shepherds of the flock," and not false shepherds. Finally, we are invited to "manifest a deep, earnest interest" in them (*Testimonies*, vol. 6, p. 78).

During dialogue conversations each side has the opportunity to speak and to listen, to remove false information and outdated stereotypes. One can repeatedly witness to one's faith and belief and learn a great deal about where other people or churches are coming from, and where they believe they are going.

There is one serendipity of dialogue that is at times overlooked. The often-unexpected blessing is that you learn to understand and *appreciate your own faith and beliefs* much more. College teachers understand what we are saying. Any college professor will tell you that in preparing and giving a college-level course, the teacher has often learned much more than the students. Having participated in several theological dialogues or conversations, I'm happy to acknowledge that my faith in the doctrines and inevitable victory of God's church of the remnant is stronger today than it was almost forty years ago, when, for the first time, I strode out onto the stage of inter-church relations as an inexperienced novice. It has been both a teaching and learning experience *par excellence*. There is a title that I have long secretly envied, which the English and later British sovereigns have enjoyed since the days of Henry VIII: "Defender of the faith."

Why did we have a dialogue with the Lutherans, and what was achieved?

We had a dialogue with the Lutheran World Federation, probably because both Lutherans and Adventists are in some ways children of Luther. Adventists hold Luther in high esteem (just read *The Great Controversy* if you have doubts!) and in some points are today more "Lutheran" than many Lutherans.

Adventists welcome contact with other Christian organizations. They are not unsociable people, with a "holier than thou" complex, nor are they theologically sectarian exclusionists. The purpose in meeting with Lutheran fellow Christians was simple and unpretentious: to achieve better mutual understanding, to break down false stereotypes, to discover each side's bases of belief, and to discover points of real and imaginary friction or disagreement. We believe that these modest goals were reached. Adventists and Lutherans met as strangers, even perhaps as suspicious newcomers, but they left as friends, as brothers and sisters who had deep spiritual fellowship together. To God be the glory.

Of course, significant doctrinal differences remain, but the participants found much in common: love for God's Word, concern for religious freedom, and above all the gospel of justification by grace through faith alone. The two sides did not just deal with the easy topics, but confronted even difficult issues such as the mark of the beast, and of course Sabbath versus Sunday.

One significant outcome has been the recommendation that Lutherans not treat the Seventh-day Adventist Church as a sect, but as a Christian World Communion. This could have important fall-out especially in countries where the Lutherans are the established majority church and where, on occasion in the past, Adventism has been treated as less than a church and not worthy of positive public notice.

 Is it possible to have dialogue or conversations with the Orthodox?

Yes, it is possible, but it moves very slowly and it takes a long time. They think in terms of decades and centuries; Adventists think in terms of days, weeks, and months. To think five years ahead is for us a long time. This is due to our eschatological time-frame, living in expectation of a soon-coming Savior. For the Orthodox, five years is a drop in the bucket of time. Adventists are pressed for time; Orthodox let time express itself.

There are two main Orthodox families. The largest group by far consists of the Eastern Orthodox Churches (Russian, Greek, Romanian and others). The second group is made up of the Oriental Orthodox family of churches (Armenians, Copts, Ethiopians, and Syrian Orthodox). The Oriental Orthodox are considered as pre-Chalcedonian churches, because they did not accept the decision of the Council of Chalcedon (A.D. 451) that there are two distinct natures in Christ. This age-old Monophysite issue is less controversial and divisive today.

So far, some Oriental Orthodox do not want to talk to Adventists, whom they accuse of not being in harmony with the teachings of the apostolic church (non-Trinitarian) and furthermore of engaging in proselytism. These accusations come largely from the leadership of the Egyptian Coptic Church, which unfortunately seems to believe, when it comes to understanding Adventist beliefs and teaching, that ignorance is bliss. Some Oriental Orthodox would be willing to talk but are held back by "hard-liners."

The Patriarchate of Constantinople, which is seen by the Eastern Orthodox as exercising a primacy of honor, has agreed in principle to have exploratory conversations with the Seventh-day Adventist Church. One helpful preliminary meeting took place in 1996, but it has not been possible for the Orthodox, because of scheduling and staff problems connected with the intensive millennial preparations and other events, to fix the time of another meeting. As has been said, "like a mighty tortoise moves the church of God," at least in segments of world Christianity. All this can be frustrating, but Jesus asks us in patience to possess our souls (see Luke 21:19, KJV).

 Should we organize with other Christians a "day of rest and worship" conference?

That is an interesting possibility. When we were ending the conversations with the Lutheran World Federation, one of the participants, who has since become a Lutheran bishop, suggested that it would be a great idea for Adventists and Lutherans to jointly sponsor an international conference in Europe dealing with promoting the day of rest and worship in a secular society.

In many Protestant countries in Europe, percentage of church attendance on Sunday is in low-middle single digits. Large churches are empty, and others have become redundant. The problem is the same in Catholic countries, and that is why Pope John Paul II wrote in May 1998 his pastoral letter on Sunday observance, calling his absent flock back to church (albeit, of course, biblically on the wrong day!).

Perhaps holding a "day of rest and worship conference" would be a good idea, and give us the opportunity to explain why our members go to church, and what is our theological and pragmatic approach. Of course, we would need to avoid in any way giving the impression that we think it makes no difference what day you observe, just so you keep one day in seven. But we should be happy that other Christians believe they can learn from *Seventh-day* Adventists how to rest and worship God.

Adventists and Roman Catholicism

 Should Seventh-day Adventists attack Catholics?

A Christian does not attack people, nor does a Christian attack churches. Attacking people or religious bodies simply because one doesn't agree with them can easily become or at least seem to be based on hate, and then perhaps be considered a hate crime. Adventists must be seen as "people who love people," and not as purveyors of hate. Unfortunately, there are misguided—sometimes unbalanced—individuals on the fringes of Adventism who see it as their task to attack Catholics, attack the pope, and attack Catholic worship and doctrine. They forget (or probably never knew) that there is much in Catholic morality and teaching that is biblical and with which we can agree.

Of course, we also know that there are substantial elements that divide us, many of them centering around the monocratic papal system, the mass as a single sacrifice together with Christ's sacrifice on the cross, and the role of the Virgin Mary and other saints. We certainly have the right and duty to positively proclaim *our* beliefs and prophetic interpretations. However, this should not involve Catholic bashing. We should be honest enough to recognize that at the Second Vatican Council, over a third of a century ago, the Catholic Church made some positive changes.

One needs to remember that much of inter-church polemic was framed during the last part of the nineteenth century when it was fashionable in regions of the U.S. to attack the Catholic Church, largely because of her intolerant record and persecuting history, unbiblical teachings, and waves of Irish and other Catholic immigrants reaching America. There was even an anti-Catholic political movement, the Know-Nothing Party. There was the propaganda slogan proclaiming opposition to "Rum, Rebellion, and Romanism." Despite such an antagonistic social setting, Ellen G. White counseled: "We should not go out of our way to make hard thrusts at the Catholics. Among the Catholics there are many who are most conscientious Christians. . . . Do not censure others; do not condemn them." She also said, "we grieve the Lord Jesus Christ by our harshness, by our unchristlike thrusts." She admitted that she herself was "hurt" by the "many decided thrusts ... against the Catholics" (*Counsels to Writers and Editors,* pp. 63, 64). Looking down the lengthening corridors of time, she predicted in 1896 that in the future "we may have less to say in some lines, in regard to the Roman power and the papacy" (Ibid., p. 65) Over a hundred years later what she said seems quite true—"in some lines."

Has the Catholic Church really changed?

The wording of this question could suggest that the Vatican might be playing a certain role just to keep its power and influence. However, we have to recognize that there are people everywhere who sincerely favor unifying Christ's body of believers, without force. Why should we not believe in the current sincerity of many religious leaders? But, this does not mean that things cannot change. Sincerity can be misguided. People can change, and influential leaders can die or leave their position. In any big organization there are many trends and individuals competing for leadership. If you watch the religious scene and listen carefully, you can see various competing forces and hear several voices, because various people have different opinions. You have also to consider strategies. There are global and local strategies. In all religious organizations, the leaders are often more open than the members.

Generally speaking, it is true that the Vatican has changed since 1962 in several areas. Is it a "profound" change? Yes and No! First, why should the Vatican change? They have a mission; they have an organization, a history, and an extraordinary presence in the world! Would the pope be eager to accept a form of presidency over the entire Christian family, to be recognized by all Christians? Would it be worth it to make some changes in the structure of the Vatican? Would the Vatican give up the primacy of the pope to please Protestants? Certainly not! Doing some of these things would divide the Roman Catholic Church.

Rome is not giving up its established dogmas. In spite of having recently changed position on evolution and hell, the Catholic Church keeps a conservative attitude on moral issues and marriage. It is keeping to its Mariology and promotion of indulgences. However, in the religious freedom area, the Roman Catholic Church during its historic Second Vatican Council turned the page on a long history of intolerance. At this council, Pope Paul VI proclaimed the declaration on religious freedom, "Dignitatis Humanae," on December 7, 1965. This change was not just window dressing, but has had a positive effect in many Catholic countries such as Italy, Spain, Portugal, Argentina, and Poland. In his address to the Diplomatic Corps January 11, 1999, Pope John Paul II said, "Time has come to ensure that everywhere in the world effective freedom of religion is guaranteed." It would have been difficult to find such a positive statement fifty years ago.

Yes, the Catholic Church has made some significant changes. However, as the French saying goes, "The more you change, the more you remain the same." The style has changed. Attitudes toward the Bible, other churches, other Christians, and Jewish people have changed. Latin is out, and the vernacular is in. Nevertheless, the old dogmas remain.

The impact of the changes undergone by the Catholic Church on the Adventist end-time scenario remains to be seen and experienced, but the changes have contributed to the increasingly significant religious and geopolitical role played by the Catholic Church today. This is part of the Adventist prophetic profile.

 Are Adventists anti-Catholic?

Among the 11 million Seventh-day Adventists, you will find some anti-Catholics; and among Catholics, you may find some anti-Adventists. In both cases, it is a wrong attitude. Adventists do not want to be portrayed as anti-Catholic. We are not anti-Catholic. In the General Conference statement, "How Seventh-day Adventists View Roman Catholicism," we read: "Seventh-day Adventists regard all men and women as equal in the sight of God. We reject bigotry against any person, regardless of race, nationality, or religious creed." Our traditional beliefs regarding eschatology are upheld, but at the same time, the possible rise of our own prejudice and bigotry is mentioned. We read, "If . . . Seventh-day Adventists fail to express love to those addressed, we do not exhibit authentic Christianity." The statement's conclusion is important: "Adventists seek to be fair in dealing with others. Thus, while we remain aware of the historical record and continue to hold our views regarding end-time events, we recognize some positive changes in recent Catholicism, and stress the conviction that many Roman Catholics are brothers and sisters in Christ."

It is a shame to read in large U.S. newspapers aggressive and unreadable ads against the pope and against the U.S. president, signed by Adventist dissidents, but using the name "Seventh-day Adventists." Many honest believers and non-believers are confusing our church with these belligerent extremists. We can disagree with a religious system or a theology without hurting people and provoking authorities. Those who are attacking other churches and lambasting believers, should read again the words of Jesus to His disciples who wanted to burn a Samaritan village: "You don't know what spirit is driving you" (Luke 9:55).

Prophetic interpretations cannot justify a lack of respect or sensitivity, and finally, a lack of Christian love. The worst thing is that those who are acting in such a non-Christian way quote Ellen G. White, claiming to be faithful to her writings. She was actually less anti-Catholic in her time than many Protestants. She warned Adventists, including preachers who use the Bible to justify their anti-Catholic statements: "I am instructed to say to our people: Be guarded. In bearing the message, make no personal thrusts at other churches, not even the Roman Catholic Church. Angels of God see in the different denominations many who can be reached only by the greatest caution. Therefore let us be careful of our words" (*Evangelism*, p. 576). She underlined the fact that Christ has to be the center of our message: "Let Christ Jesus be exalted! Keep to the affirmative of truth." She added: "Let the Word of God, which is the truth, tell the story of the inconsistency of those in error." Even ministers may forget this wise advice. Why? Do we perhaps receive more financial support when not speaking "the truth in tones and words of love"? The following quotation of Ellen G. White is valuable to remember before every public speaking engagement. She says, "Let not our ministers follow their own impulses in denouncing and exposing the 'mysteries of iniquity.' Upon these themes silence is eloquence." Truth should be proclaimed with the hope of making friends; the intent should not be to make enemies.

In reading these quotations, we should not forget that they were written during a very anti-Catholic time in the U.S. Of course, during the same time in Europe, Catholics were strongly anti-Protestant. Ellen G. White kept *Christ* in the center of her teaching.

Will Seventh-day Adventists and Catholics ever have a dialogue?

Who knows. In the past, quite understandably, the attitude has been "never the twain shall meet." There are no current plans. Of course, informal conversations have taken place on occasion between Catholics and Adventists when they have happened to meet each other at conferences. One thing I have discovered (and it came somewhat as a surprise), is that at various interchurch meetings we find it easier to agree with the Catholics than with liberal Protestant theologians, in regard especially to moral standards or conduct, sociopolitical involvement, and ecumenical activism.

The Vatican has not proposed official conversations with the Seventh-day Adventist Church; neither have we. When the Church published a statement on Catholics in 1997, one Catholic official in the Vatican asked, "Why do Adventists believe we want to persecute them?" He remarked that the Vatican has never pushed for the persecution of the Seventh-day Adventist Church. Many Catholics are aware of *The Great Controversy* and are shocked by some of our literature and the way we sometimes picture the Vatican in advertising or oral presentations. One Monsignor suggested, "Why not have a discussion about this issue?" Quite a challenge. Would this be our opportunity to explain our vision of the great controversy?

The Reformers never refused an opportunity to share what the Bible teaches. We believe we have received special understanding regarding the eschatological future. Should we be ready to share it with others, including those who are specifically concerned? Of course, it has to be done in an intelligent and understandable way, not by using code words that are mysterious and unclear. We are not against people or individuals, but we believe that there is a type of organization which can be in opposition to the gospel and dangerous to religious freedom; many other Christians believe this and are able to grasp an intelligent, flexible explanation of our prophetic interpretation.

Could it not be helpful to discuss together our understanding and support of religious liberty, our concept of worldwide evangelism, and the related problem of proselytism? Would it not be of practical value to discuss with Catholic representatives the actual problems Adventists face in certain historically Catholic countries or regions? Would it not be of merit to explain and hear where it is felt that unfair, discriminatory, or aggressive tactics are being used? No one is perfect, and we can all learn and improve, aiming at true Christian maturity in and through Jesus Christ. But, perhaps we are too optimistic and asking for too much. God knows.

 Does the General Conference have an ambassador to the Vatican?

A church organization cannot have an ambassador to the "Holy See" or Vatican; only governments can do so. The Holy See wishes to be recognized as a state, and governments that recognize the statehood of the Vatican establish diplomatic relations and send an ambassador to the Holy See. A church may have a mission or a representative in Rome, such as the Archbishop of Canterbury has, but not an ambassador. The General Conference of Seventh-day Adventists has no ambassador or representative to the Vatican, and there are no plans to have one. In fact, when the United States government decided to form diplomatic relations with the Holy See, the General Conference opposed this arrangement, and Dr. Beach testified twice before Congress and spoke on television in opposition, because of the American concept of separation of church and state, and because the Holy See is essentially a church.

Having no official bilateral relations does not mean that there is no contact at all. On occasion, Adventist Church officials meet representatives at the Holy See in Geneva, New York, or elsewhere, including sometimes in Rome, usually in connection with some other meeting. We have common interests to defend, such as religious freedom, marriage, humanitarian work, and human rights. We have ongoing, regular relations with many governments and organizations, but those with the Vatican are more sporadic and ad hoc.

Is there a global Roman Catholic evangelistic campaign specifically targeting Seventh-day Adventists?

Beginning in 1999, a document started circulating that probably originated somewhere in Latin America, perhaps Central America. It purports to represent an organized ten-point program (or even more than ten points) from the Vatican specifically aimed at evangelizing Seventh-day Adventists. As far as we can tell, the document is spurious. It is poorly put together and sounds rather primitive. Some of the language looks more like garbled Adventist terminology and not the way Catholics express themselves. The Vatican itself has stated it has no reason to believe the document is authentic. Our impression is that the document has been concocted or changed by enemies on the fringes or outside our church.

Having said all this, it must be made clear that Catholics have every right to evangelize any region or people-group in the world. This is a principle of religious liberty. Furthermore, any church that is losing members to other churches has the right to use legitimate evangelistic means to protect itself and try to stop the membership hemorrhage. Quite a number of Catholics, often only nominal members, have become Adventists. Any local Catholic bishop or member worth his salt would be expected to be concerned by such a development and react in his local diocese. There is, however, no creditable evidence of a worldwide Vatican sponsored campaign aiming at specifically winning Seventh-day Adventists.

In the *General Conference Working Policy* 0/100, we affirm our right and our divine commission to call the gospel "to the attention of all peoples everywhere." While we believe we have a message of present gospel truth for everyone, we also acknowledge that other churches, including the Church of Rome, have this same religious liberty right in civil society. As the saying goes, what is good for the goose is also good for the gander. Religious liberty is important to the goose, especially when she is laying golden evangelistic eggs.

 Do Adventists trouble the Vatican and thus represent a major concern for the Catholic Church?

Some Adventists think that Rome has its sights fixed on the SDA Church. This indicates an inclination toward egocentrism. Such a view does not represent a balanced or healthy attitude, but rather a kind of obsession. Many Adventists are certainly more focused on the Vatican than the Vatican is on Adventists. Highlighting in Adventist public evangelism prophetic interpretations in which the papacy plays a sinister role, does trouble Catholics. The Vatican, however, is more concerned by the extraordinary growth of the Pentecostals, especially in Latin America. In China there appear to be more Pentecostals than Catholics. The Pentecostal world membership has been numbered somewhere between 300-500 million.

In its search of unity, the Vatican has its traditional counterparts: the World Council of Churches, the Anglicans, and the Orthodox Churches. Now Rome finds it important to build bridges with Pentecostals and other Evangelicals. Things have dramatically changed during this last decade. Traditional Protestant churches have been losing members, and the Evangelicals have been growing rapidly and have become in many areas the strongest group among the

Protestants. You cannot work for unity of the Christian Church by ignoring this fact. The Roman Catholic Church sees the Evangelicals, including Pentecostals, as its most vigorous and growing religious competitors, not Seventh-day Adventists.

Has the General Conference president met with the pope?

No. The pope meets many people—thousands and thousands in general audiences, and small groups or individuals in special or private audiences. Thus, it is not unusual for him to meet leaders or heads of churches. It happens that Adventists attending certain meetings have met the pope. Dr. Jean Nussbaum met with Pope Pious XII several times in the '50s to talk about religious freedom. Dr. Beach has also met several popes. Our leaders in Rome and others have had this opportunity, but never the General Conference president. Because the pope is not an "ordinary" religious leader, and for that matter, neither is the General Conference president, such a meeting could send an ambiguous message and be misinterpreted, and there is no demand for such a meeting from either side. Adventist understanding of the papal system and history is rooted in our prophetic understanding; we cannot and dare not overlook this.

Did the Seventh-day Adventist Church give a medal to the pope?

Here are the facts that contradict some of the mythology which has circulated: In 1977 there was a meeting of Christian World Communions in Rome. On this occasion, fifteen church executives had an audience with the pope. This is a normal protocol when church leaders meet in Rome, in view of the primordial role of the pope as leader of hundreds of millions of Catholics. In the group was one Seventh-day Adventist who was serving at that time as public affairs and religious liberty director in the Northern Europe-West Africa Division. When one meets with the pope, it is customary for him to give one of his medals to a guest as a memento of the meeting. Wondering how he could respond as a person and a witness, the Adventist decided, on his own initiative, to present Pope Paul VI with a short picture-and-message book and one of the medals (or medallions) available in the General Conference to give to leading personalities when meeting with them. Thus, the medal was not struck specifically for the pope.

The medal shows the Adventist and Sabbath message on both sides: "Behold He Cometh," and "every eye shall see Him." The Ten Commandments are represented by Roman numerals, but the fourth is written out, "Remember the Sabbath day to keep it holy." The pope made one interesting little comment: "Your medal is better than mine!" In this case, and with due humility, we agree.

Giving a medal as a memento to the pope did not mean "wandering" after the papacy, anymore than the pope giving a medal meant he was "wandering" after the Seventh-day Adventist Church. We need to be aware of the opportunities involved in public relations. Sometimes they are frequent; other times they are rare.

 How will the Catholic Church answer and deal with its religious competition?

It would, of course, be rather pretentious to claim to know the thinking and plans of Catholic leaders. However, we do have biblical prophetic guidance and past experience to help us.

There are two possible answers we would like to suggest:

1. The first answer is for Catholicism to strongly defend its traditional position and hold on by all means to its advantages, which is risky. You can win, but you can also lose. Staying on the defensive means you may be tempted to use the power of the state to help you. Fighting means you can lose control of your people and have war: a religious war,

including the risk of alienation and persecution! History teaches us that the dominant church has often used the secular power to fight its competitors. Of course, acting in this way would destroy the current image of the Catholic Church as a leading advocate of human rights and religious freedom.

2. The second approach to the non-Catholic denominations is to try to renew and improve your own church or programs and build bridges and work for peace, which is the Christian way. This means to accept religious freedom for all and to promote some form, though perhaps limited, of separation between church and state. The Vatican gives little indication of wanting to change its commitment to human rights and religious freedom.

The present indication is that Catholicism is leaning toward the second answer. Does this mean that the Vatican will never change? Not at all! But we have to be honest enough to recognize change— what is the case today, what is good, and what is wrong. We have to make a clear distinction between facts and perspectives, between present and future. We must also be able to *come to grips with the present* as it is now, and not only delve into the past or concentrate on speculating about final events.

 Will the Vatican be faithful to religious freedom?

Muslims do not accept the right of a Muslim to change his religion. Hindus are concerned about the number of conversions to Christianity. Orthodox churches fear inroads by Evangelicals. Can the Vatican allow Catholics to leave their church? Will a church of nearly one billion members, with a strong influence on many governments, be faithful to religious freedom?

First, we have to say that since Vatican II, respect for other religions and for religious liberty is a fact in most Catholic countries.

This does not mean that it will last forever. People change, concepts change, and times change. In case of a strong threat to its dominant position, the Vatican would be tempted to work through secular governments to protect its position and interests. The Medieval Church, the Inquisition, could return in subtle ways.

About twenty years ago, I had an interesting experience. In Rome I met with a Catholic Cardinal who had become friendly with me after I had arranged for him to receive medical treatment at one of our health care institutions in Scandinavia. He was now the secretary of the Vatican "Congregation for the Doctrine of the Faith." But remember that until about 1900, this congregation was still called the "Holy Office of the Inquisition"! I asked him, now that the Catholic Church had accepted religious liberty in 1965, whether it would be possible for the Catholic Church to abandon religious liberty and return to the former position. He answered without hesitation, "The change is irreversible!" That was his clear opinion, but people change, and so do circumstances and situations.

Let us accuse no one of intolerance without strong evidence. We should never forget that many Catholics have defended religious freedom. True, we have a good record, but we do not have the monopoly in this domain. How many sincere Catholics have defended us in several cases! How many loyal Catholics gave their life to defend the right to believe! They are children of God. In Catholicism, as in every group and religion, you find different opinions. We have to admit that and thank the Lord when pro-religious freedom leaders are in power. We must never forget that this can change. We can disagree with several doctrines of the Roman Catholic Church, but we must recognize positive aspects about their religion.

Freedom is for all. We do not wish to join a large Christian church under the moral authority of the pope, but we recognize the right of others to do that. In the same way, we want to be free to follow another direction and free to share our beliefs. People can argue about theology, but when someone is persecuted because of his or her faith, the right to religious freedom has been denied. If an organization persecutes people because of their belief in Christ, it is anti-Christian. What makes the difference is the act.

 Have Jesuits infiltrated the General Conference?

This may sound like a silly question, but from time to time people do inquire whether there are Jesuit spies in the General Conference World Headquarters of the Seventh-day Adventist Church. Someone telephoned recently and asked, "Can you convince me that there are no Jesuit spies working in the General Conference?" The answer to that person's question is "probably not." Some people are conspiracy oriented and are attracted by interpretations (sometimes outlandish and void of sound biblical exegesis) regarding plagues, marching armies, false prophets, deceptive intrigues, images, marks, numerology, secret numbers, beasts, eternal torment, and Armageddon. All these are part of the biblical prophetic scenario, which people twist at their own peril.

In the United States, during the McCarthy period of the '50s, some saw hidden communists in every aspect of American life. A few Adventists apparently imagine a Jesuit behind every bush, forgetting for one that the Jesuit order is considerably reduced in size, having now only about 22,000 members. Furthermore, you don't become a Jesuit priest or brother by simply taking a quick correspondence course of a few months, or even residential study lasting a couple of years. It takes many years of study and formation to join the Jesuit order.

Another simple point needs to be made: What purpose would there be in spying on the General Conference? Every significant thing we do is transparent and not secret, except at times when dealing with personnel issues on nominating or other committees, or when sensitive personal reputations, capacities, and character are in play. Even when it recently became necessary to make a change in the General Conference leadership, the church, through the *Adventist*

Review and her world divisions, kept the membership very well informed, despite the delicate and unpleasant issues involved. Our policies are voted in open Annual Councils. Our departmental activities are openly promoted and evangelistic activities are advertised. We are not plotting against people, other churches, or governments. Everyone who reads our books, magazines, or news releases knows what we are doing and can discover our priorities. We have no secrets. If there are any, I don't know what they are—and I have been a member of the General Conference Executive Committee for 40 years, and my father was on the Committee for 28 years before I had the privilege of joining. So, we have a long collective memory.

Of course, you cannot *prove* that there are no Jesuits in the General Conference. There are things you cannot prove and really *don't need to prove*. How can you *prove* that Mother Teresa, or anyone for that matter, did not steal or commit adultery? You can't and don't need to, when their reputations are as solid as the Rock of Gibraltar. If individuals have any credible evidence pointing to Jesuits in the General Conference, let them come forward and provide the proof. They have been asked to do this, and have never been able to do so, because there is no evidence. Let us not be distracted by conspiracy red herrings.

 Did the pope state in his May 1998 pastoral letter on Sunday worship that the only true Christians are Sunday keepers?

This is a good example of people manipulating a text to support their desires and wishful thinking. The pope was writing to Catholics, especially that great majority which does not go to church on Sunday. A good Catholic is obviously a Sunday keeper. However, it is not accurate to say the pope states that all true Christians are Sunday keepers. Maybe the pope thinks that this is the case, but that is not what he wrote. Perhaps some would be happy if the text read that way, to confirm their vision of the end, but he did not write that. What the pope said is, Catholics should observe Sunday as their day of rest and worship and attend mass. That is what we would expect him to say to his members. If we claim to have and to preach the truth, we have to say the truth. We cannot build an argument simply on what people might be thinking but not saying. A good test that every Adventist should ask: "Is it the truth?"

 Are the Third Millennium ceremonies a triumphal climax for the Vatican?

It was a test for ecumenical relations. The Vatican would have liked to convene non-Catholic leaders for a meeting with the pope in the year 2000. SDA representatives heard that the invitations were being given. We saw the Protestant leaders slow to respond to such invitations. It was probably felt that a big meeting in Palestine or elsewhere with all the leaders at the left and right side of the pope would have created misunderstandings. The media could have exploited this event as tacit recognition of papal supremacy. There is little doubt that among many Protestants and Orthodox, there would have been a negative reaction. Others will respond favorably.

The figure of 30 million "pilgrims" to Rome in the year 2000 has been mentioned. The Vatican, the Diocese of Rome, and the city of Rome have been making great preparations. In July 1999, the Italian Protestant Federation published a revealing document titled "Italian Protestants and the Holy Year." In the first two pages the document underlines a commitment to ecumenism, and then on page 3 the document states a disappointment, mentioning the solemn papal letter promulgated November 29, 1998 for the induction of the Great Jubilee, *Incarnationis Mysterium*. Why the disappointment? "In this document the whole theology on indulgences is re-proposed, against which Luther had arisen, followed by all the other reformers" (*Italian Protestants and the Holy Year*, Rome, May 11, 1999, The Council of the Federation of Protestant Churches in Italy, p. 3). The document also laments the enormous Italian media campaign focusing on the Vatican. It says, "The continual takeover of 'spaces' in the public sector has already started . . . totally unthinkable in a lay state, that seeks to guide everything to a single religious and cultural organic project." (Ibid., p. 3) The Protestants in Italy decided to "celebrate the second millennium of the birth of Christ with sobriety, but we will not participate in any manifestation conceived within the celebrations of the Holy Year" (Ibid., p. 4).

Adventists have also declined to participate in the Holy Year millennial celebrations or events organized by the Vatican. The main reason for doing so is very simple: for Adventists, the birth of Christ two thousand years ago must be the center focus, together with the promise of His soon return. At any celebratory event the pope attends with all the media hoopla, the pope inevitably becomes the center of attention, and Christ is eclipsed.

Adventists and Final Events

 Is a National Sunday law being proposed?

Not now, but the matter of a Sunday law has always been an important consideration among Adventists. It is part of our subculture. Our Church grew up with this threat in the U.S. In the last part of the nineteenth century, we had to face several bills in favor of a national Sunday law, and even a proposal for a constitutional amendment. By the grace of God and the U.S. Constitution, we won and this amendment was defeated. In our prophetic interpretation of the end time, a Sunday law will be passed, the Constitution will be amended, and Sabbath keepers will be persecuted. The end will knock at the door and Christ's return will become a reality.

As there is no bill that could be qualified as a Sunday law, some Adventists are impatient and almost try to create Sunday laws! By working for the church in the Department of Public Affairs and Religious Liberty, we occupy the best position to make our people aware when such developments take place. We do not like to engage in prognosticating speculations. This would discredit our ministry within the church and among governments and international organizations. Others have done so, and they are no longer taken seriously. But be sure that when the time comes, we will react and strongly oppose an oppressive national Sunday law.

We must also recognize that Sunday laws have long existed in several countries in the world. Switzerland has a very strong Sunday law. But it does not force us to go either to church on Sunday or not to go to church on Saturday. It is a social law with a religious origin. The Sunday law we Adventists are vigorously opposed to, will force us not to go to church on Saturday. It would be a bad law essentially, not so much because it would promote Sunday, but because it would persecute those who have a day of rest other than Sunday.

I am always perturbed when I travel in countries where our members are under discriminating pressure from the main church or are being persecuted, and they ask questions about the Sunday law in the U.S.! They receive false information from Adventists or former Adventists who have lost their judgment. The U.S. is portrayed as an oppressive country where Adventists are being persecuted. It is true that Adventists can have problems in their work place and in schools over observing the Sabbath. But they go to court and defend their rights. We have lawyers helping them, and we often win. In many countries in the world, the right to go to court for religious liberty reasons is practically non-existent. When you are a member of a religious minority, in many countries, you are a second-class citizen. There is little doubt that a repressive Sunday law would end the American democracy founded by people who believed in both civil and religious freedom. The lamb would become a dragon. The metamorphosis will have been completed.

 Does the Church still believe in prophecy?

We hear this question from some members who are disappointed because they feel church pastors do not speak often enough about last day events. Many dissidents claim they are meeting this lack of prophetic emphasis. Of course, the church still believes in prophecy. Of course, the Department of Public Affairs and Religious Liberty believes in prophecy. Prophetic interpretation gives us the right understanding of the time and of events. But believing in prophecy does not mean misusing prophecy as a spectacular tool to attract people and their money. We must not manipulate prophecies only to please some people. We should not create prophetic events based on today's newspaper headlines. This may momentarily get people's attention, but a backlash follows later when disappointment sets in. People resent being misled. Disillusioned members tend to leave the church.

We have to be honest and serious in studying bills, laws, conflicts, events, and statements. There are many facts today that confirm our prophetic interpretation, so it is not necessary to create shaky evidence and produce confusion. We saw how the pope's pastoral letter on Sunday was used in a tendentious way, only to try to prove that some prophetic interpretation was right. Truth does not need sensational speculation to give it credence. God is the God of truth and Jesus is the Lord of truth.

 Is the end-time prophetic scenario obsolete?

Not at all! In studying the present through prophetic vision, we can see many signs confirming our beliefs. While this is not the place to go into details of the prophetic end-time scenario, we can see the outline coming into focus. Never has the papacy been so respected in geopolitical terms. Pope John Paul II is probably considered by many to be one of the pivotal, great men at the beginning of this century. In a world of moral decadence, he is seen as the key defender of moral values, life, the family, and marriage without compromise. When we think of great ecclesiastic strength, we tend to think of the papacy and this pope. When we think of a unique superpower, we must think of the United States of America. Who can challenge these powers? By saying this, does not our prophetic interpretation receive confirmation? But further issues need to be identified and classified, and numerous steps still need to be climbed.

We are now living in what has been called the "global village." All parts of the world are linked together through cyberspace, political institutions (including the United Nations), multinational industries, global religious bodies, and international courts of justice to pursue crimes against humanity. All this "globality" is a necessary setting in order for final events to take place, because the end of the great controversy will transpire on a global scale. Worldwide religious conflict and persecution presuppose some form of world-government and worldwide religious authority. Both the UN and the papacy have staked out claims in these domains.

For several decades all seemed quiet on the Sunday law front. More recently, several countries have experienced tension and controversies in this area as the opponents and proponents of "closed Sundays" have clashed. In addition, the 1998 papal pastoral letter on Sunday observance has helped place the issue on the public agenda.

We must be wise enough not to confuse and mix past, present, and future, or be blinded by forgetting past events or closing our eyes and minds to new and surprising facts. Very often the consummation of prophecy is much larger and more inclusive than previously envisioned by human beings. The fulfillment of end-time prophecy will present indeed a beautiful plenitude that may well go beyond the anticipation of finite minds. God is not the prisoner of our limited prophetic interpretation, no matter how biblically based it is. He is the Master of both history and prophecy. He is the One who will decide when "these things begin to come to pass" (Luke 21:28) and when time is over. In the meantime, "we have this hope, hope in the coming of the Lord."

When will persecution begin?

You can never be sure. In some places, it is already here. 1 Thessalonians 5:3 highlights the suddenness and unexpected nature of trouble and persecution: "For when they shall say, peace and safety; then sudden destruction cometh upon them . . . ." Let us watch.

We can be persecuted for our faith at any moment. You can live in a country where religious freedom is officially protected, but be persecuted in the work place, or at school, or even at home. Of course, we must differentiate between difficulties and persecution. Problems may be annoying, but they are not persecution. Persecution can also happen as an indirect effect of a large national crisis. The context changes, new rules are imposed, and you find yourself out of step and in conflict. Persecution is rarely a straightforward policy or a direct cause. All the more, it is necessary to be alert, analyze things, and do all that you can to protect freedom.

If you study the story of persecution, you can see more or less the same germinating process:

1. A group that is different
2. Rumors or false information circulating about this group
3. Classification of the group as potentially dangerous or already a menace
4. Crisis in the nation or establishment
5. Accusation and defamation
6. Persecution

It seems that when people, including authorities, feel insecure, they need a scapegoat to exorcise their fears. Some countries in Western Europe are already at Step 3. But we must stay confident because we understand the issue and process, and we know that in any case, God will protect His people. Creating pressure on religious minorities who focus on the end of time can have negative results. Outrage can easily transform a peaceful group into a belligerent anti-social minority. The trap for the group is to cultivate and enhance its isolation by burning bridges with society. Falling into this trap, the group will be totally neutralized, perhaps not destroyed, but caged in an ecclesiastical blockhouse. Adventists must avoid such a fortress mentality.

Q **Is there a risk in evaluating or prejudging events and people through Adventist apocalyptic interpretation?**

Yes, the temptation is always there. The interpretation can be helpful and illuminating. But we also have prejudices (at times, strong prejudices) that can color our interpretations. The conspiracy syndrome affects a number of Adventists around the world, making it difficult to be balanced, objective, and able to analyze facts and events. As each United States president leaves office, we accept the fact that he was not as dangerous as some thought. Adventists also believe that a pope will push for a global persecution against Sabbath keepers. When each pope dies, we admit that he was not the one, but will the next pope be "the one"?

If you have the time to read what Adventists have written over the years interpreting emphatically the role assigned to popes, U.S. presidents, and other rulers since the 1850s, you will understand the danger of prejudging prophetic events. We often forget that no one should judge people before they have committed a crime. We should make a clear distinction between function, system, and persons. We should be able to make a distinction between facts and interpretations, and between present, past, and future. We should also learn to pay tribute to those religious leaders and politicians who protect our freedoms and our peace. Greater care in interpreting events and developments, less judgment, and more thanks will give us a better image and will make us better witnesses for Christ.

Could the International Religious Freedom Act be used against Adventists?

The Commission may propose appropriate sanctions against a country that officially persecutes a religious minority, though one wonders whether this will actually happen—certainly not often. What kind of sanctions would, for example, the U.S. government take against Saudi Arabia? Politics can neutralize the goodwill of people, but we shall see what the future holds. The purpose of the law is to promote and to protect religious freedom for all, especially to defend religious minorities who are persecuted. I cannot imagine that such a law could be used against Adventists or someone else, without violating its own purpose and text. About the sanctions, Ambassador Seiple has said the new law "was written to promote religious freedom, not necessarily to target a particular country or region—or certainly not a particular faith" (RIPNet News: April 26, 1999). Adventists who are U.S. citizens should be proud to have such a law and to be part of a country that stands for this great principle of religious freedom.

 Could an alliance between the Vatican and the United States operate against religious freedom?

The progressivists had a significant influence for change at the Second Vatican Council. During the pontificate of John Paul II, they have been under pressure from a new conservative force. In many ways, this steel-clad pope restored order and discipline to the Catholic Church. His role in the collapse of totalitarian communism in Poland, with a ripple effect in other countries of the eastern block, influenced developments in the Soviet Union. The "Washington-Vatican alliance" came about because both the United States and the Vatican were interested in defeating the "evil empire" of communism. This same alliance worked in South America against the left-wing partisans of the theology of liberation. It is interesting to notice how the two superpowers, one political and the other religious, worked together to achieve a common political goal.

What about the future? In terms of geopolitics, it would appear that Islam, especially Islamic fundamentalism, is becoming of increasing concern to both Rome and Washington. At the other end of the spectrum, secularization is viewed as a great threat by the Vatican because its effects are strongly seen in countries traditionally considered as "Christian," many of them with a large Catholic majority. In the United States, the Christian right—concerned by the rising tide of anti-Christian secular influences in society—has been warming up politically to Catholicism.

A third threat could be seen as coming from radical opponents within Christianity, who refuse the ecumenical vision of unity and keep evangelizing or proselytizing in "Catholic" countries. The so called "sects" or "cults" are not spared by the Catholic media. More and more the border between "sects" and "churches" is determined by the position on ecumenism and proselytism.

For those who believe in the principle of religious freedom, it will be interesting to see the following:

1. How the Vatican will react in Latin America to the continuing growth of the Evangelicals, including Seventh-day Adventists.

2. Whether the "Holy Alliance" will be resurrected to work against such minorities, as it worked against totalitarian communism. If this were to be the case, it would indicate that the United States is giving up its past and current belief in religious liberty for all people everywhere and its belief in separation of church and state.

3. Whether in the 21st Century, South America will become a testing ground for Rome and Washington regarding religious freedom. Another test of the "Alliance" could be the

Muslim world and its challenges to both American foreign policy and the global outreach of Catholicism. This "globality" should lead Seventh-day Adventists to avoid a centrist outlook that focuses only on United States internal politics, and to adopt a more sweeping geopolitical vision of coming events.

 What can we do to face last day events and difficulties?

First of all, we need to be of good cheer, for when you are on God's side, you are inevitably on the winning side. True, difficulties and persecution can come any time, anywhere. Rumors about a religious minority can spread rapidly and unexpectedly, and it can be targeted by the media, politicians, church leaders, and the police as a public enemy.

The story of Esther teaches us that God protects His minority people. He has His own individuals in the right high places to help His church. We need to remember that the people of God are not limited to those listed on church membership books. What can we do and what should we not do?

1. Trust in God. He is the Master of History. He is the victorious Savior and He will protect us.

2. Do nothing to provoke persecution. We should not support those who deliberately attack other churches or religions during public meetings. It is a poor strategy, which gives us bad publicity and gives our members a lot of problems; it produces a lot of enemies.

3. Do not use rumors or sensationalism to feed the blind faith or wishful thinking of your brothers and sisters. Fear is not the best means to nurture spirituality.

4. Be honest and careful when you quote or share information that could be interpreted in a wrong way. Screen all infor-

mation before sharing it.

5. Be proactive. Don't wait to be persecuted before organizing a local chapter of the International Religious Liberty Association and meeting with authorities and religious leaders.

6. Work through the church network for advice and information.

7. Be faithful and ask God to help you and His people to become good disciples, whether free or persecuted. In our travels through life, persecution is neither the end nor the goal, but a challenge we may have to meet. We have a hope, and we know that Jesus will return, and by faith we know that we have a bright future. Jesus said to His disciples, the person "who stands firm to the end will be saved" (Matthew 10:22) and will enter into the joy of the Lord.

As Adventists, we know why we are on earth. We have a mission to fulfill, in easy or difficult times, until the Lord comes.

If you enjoyed this book, you'll enjoy these as well:

Like a Fire in My Bones

Clifford Goldstein. The author's most important and passionate messages. The best of what he has written over the last 20 years touches on topics such as end times, religious persecution, the judgment, and more.
0-8163-1580-9. Paperback. US$12.99, Cdn$19.49.

One Nation Under God?

Clifford Goldstein. Does Bible prophecy predict the failure of American democracy near the end of time? Is it already happening in our country? In a book that reaches back into American history and snatches events from today's headlines, Clifford Goldstein warns us that our freedom is more precious—and more precarious—than we think.
0-8163-1308-3. US$10.99, Cdn$16.49.

Order from your ABC by calling **1-800-765-6955**, or get online and shop our virtual store at **www.adventistbookcenter.com**.
  • Read a chapter from your favorite book.
  • Order online.
  • Sign up for e-mail notices on new products.